Noah's Vessel

TRIGUEIRINHO

Noah's Vessel

Shasti Association

Copyright © 2021 Jose Trigueirinho Netto

The profits generated from sales of books by Trigueirinho and his associates will be used to support the non-profit activities of the Shasti Association to disseminate their work.

Original Title in Portuguese:

A NAVE DE NOÉ – Sao Paulo, Brazil: Editora Pensamento.
Copyright © 1989 by José Trigueirinho Netto

Cover photo by John David Cutrell

Cataloging-in-Publication data

Trigueririnho Netto, José
Noah's Vessel
Trigueirinho. – Mount Shasta, CA, Shasti Association 2rd edition, 2021
138 p.
ISBN: 978-1-948430-10-4
Library of Congress Control Number: 2021930533
1. Occult science
2. Spirituality
3. New Age
I. Title.

English language rights reserved

Shasti Association
P.O. Box 318
Mt. Shasta, CA 96067-0318
editorial@shasti.org
www.shasti.org

The keys to the kingdom were hidden: they did not enter nor did they let pass those who desired to enter.

"But you are to be as wise as serpents and as simple as doves."

A Third Century Book

Contents

To the Reader 9

FIRST PART

Seeking Evidence—an Obstacle to Inner Knowledge 13
Awakening from Dense Sleep 21
Revelations for Vessel Sojourners 27
New Situations for Rescued Individuals 31
In the Vessel 39
What the Sojourners Envision 45
The Virgin of Ether 51
Letting Go of the Guardians 57
Samana and Other Noahs 69

SECOND PART

Those Who Do Not Listen 81
Other Floods 87

THIRD PART

Questions from Students 101

Glossary 109

References 119

Works by Trigueirinho 123

To the Reader

Humans are presently developing their right side consciousness, the part of their being which gives them the ability, never before experienced, to perceive inner reality without depending on external information that is subject to the level of evolution and the conditions of civilization in general. "Be careful not to be deceived," warns an apocryphal Gospel.[1] "Do not be disheartened if you cannot answer what they ask you, because I will give you the voice and wisdom which your opponents will not be able to dispute."

We offer this book as a contribution to the development of this intuitive ability and as an encouragement for each one to seek his or her confirmations within. Some facts we present here would be impossible to prove except through an inmost feeling that may emerge from deep within each reader's own self at the appropriate moment attesting to their veracity. Here a being such as Plato could be as close to your inner world as a neighbor is to you on the physical level. Continents such as ancient Atlantis could be as

---

[1] See Glossary.

real to you as those on a current world map. Without this kind of flexibility, reading this book would be to no avail.

After the series of books concluding with *In Search of Synthesis*[2] that brought a cycle of work to completion, we realized that it would be timely to publish something which would evoke in the conscious universe of those seeking the unknown, a subtle and non-material atmosphere that would further the expansion of their perceptions.

We have attempted to do this, aware that in our current critical times people will need to re-awaken to their relationship with supraphysical energies, with Beings and with Entities that can come to their assistance when they will feel totally at a loss in the three-dimensional levels of consciousness.

Now is the time for Noah's vessel to appear on Earth; the problems created by this civilization have gone far beyond the bounds of common human capacity to solve them.

TRIGUEIRINHO

---

[2] See works by Trigueirinho on page 123.

FIRST PART

Seeking Evidence–an Obstacle to Inner Knowledge

For centuries the Bible has exerted a powerful influence on various levels of human consciousness, especially in regard to the uplifting of feelings and the development of will in humankind. Notwithstanding the diverse interpretations of this sacred book by different religions, its faulty translations and all the misconceptions that people have construed in regard to it throughout time, the Bible is still undeniably prevalent.

Organized religions have taken upon themselves the safeguarding and ownership of concepts set forth by the Bible. For this reason, whenever possible, Blavatsky[3] presented other interpretations in order to help free ordinary people from the dominance of these institutions which have adhered rigorously to the views held by a few dogmatic translators and theologians. Rudolf Steiner[4] also gave humanity a different insight into biblical knowledge.

---

[3] See Glossary.
[4] See Glossary.

Through his books and lectures related to the subject, one can perceive that the wisdom of the Bible need not be limited to what is written down or to what is generally known.

For example, in the traditional text two names are given for God: "Elohim" and "Jehovah." No matter how hard some theologians and historians attempt to explain it rationally, the difference between these two names is not clear, nor will it be as long as we limit ourselves to studies based on the dead letter, or on allegedly historical data.

Could the Bible be more than a book? Could it be understood on different levels? Could it be considered as an energy impulse that resonates infinitely within those who read it? Would the Bible become more accessible if people really obeyed the spiritual laws that it reveals? Yet, how can we assimilate what is in the Bible when we do not even abide by the Ten Commandments? How can people understand the deeper meaning of the Bible when they are unable to comply with the simple Decalogue representing the more external and concrete levels of Cosmic Law, a Law which contains so many meanings unknown to the majority and which requires even greater individual effort in the quest for Truth?

In order to solve the dilemma of the terms "Elohim" and "Jehovah," some translators decided to replace these with "God" and "Lord," without following any criteria that could clearly differentiate them, which indicates both their ignorance and how little they lived the spiritual law. However, the limitations of the current editions of the Bible became evident as *The Secret Doctrine* was revealed by Blavatsky, as Steiner presented more reflective points of view of the four known Gospels and of the Old Testament, and also as secret manuscripts formerly considered apocryphal were gradually made public. In his book, *Discover Yourself*,[5] (also entitled *The Inner Reality*), Paul Brunton describes how a group of men declaring to be imbued with the "Holy Spirit," selected the passages that make up today's New Testament. Those men introduced elements which, from a purely material point of view, have governed the world for centuries. At the time this selection was made, it was even said that the pages fell into place on their own under the eyes of those compilers of the New Testament.

Nevertheless, through the energy of Love-Wisdom, which guides the destiny of our solar system, other perspectives have emerged and today the question of spiritual Laws is more enlightened. We should try to see the history of the salvation of humankind—as old as the Earth itself—from a point of view free of dogmas. It has always been known that this planet would be a repository for remnants from different galaxies and thus it would harbor forces that were still not reconciled, forces coming from earlier solar systems or from previous incarnations of this galaxy. Humanity, in turn, was made up of essences coming from different parts of the cosmos. Consequently, ever since the very beginning of this world, humanity has always been disunited.

The cyclic time has come for this disarray to be straightened out; now is the time for "Noah's ark" to reappear. Just as at the time of the flood (or of the floods), the ark could have been a symbol of intraterrestrial[6] civilizations, today's space vessels could be considered symbols of extraterrestrial or intergalactic civilizations,

---

[5] Paul Brunton, *Discover Yourself*, Revised Edition [Newburyport, MA: Weiser Books], 1985

[6] **Intraterrestrial.** This refers to the supraphysical and not to the physical level.

which, together with the intraterrestrial civilizations, are cooperating in the transmigration of rescuable humans of the surface of the Earth. We are using the term "vessel,"[7] which today is more widespread than "ark," so as to make it easier to understand the events that are still to occur, or that are already taking place, albeit not yet on a global level. Currently, interplanetary, intergalactic and intraterrestrial space vessels are serving the Earth. Intra-oceanic vessels are also active, although they are not seen as frequently as the others. Among all of these which we call "vessels," "Noah's vessel" is the largest and is in charge of directing the transmigration of a part of humanity from the surface of the Earth.

◆ ◆ ◆

Rudolf Steiner says that the only proper interpreter of the Bible is the one who on his own is capable of reaching the same truths presented therein. Furthermore, only someone who is capable of creating wisdom from within his or her own inner being can be considered a true authority on the Bible.

With regard to the apparent contradictions found in the official texts (usually compiled by those whom Christ referred to as "the blind leading the blind"), one could say that the Bible, like any book inspired by supraphysical levels, is only comprehensible to those who penetrate the spiritual-evolutionary meaning of the world, both in its external and its inner dimensions. An inspired text is to be read, meditated upon and drawn into our inner world and not to be entrusted only to our earthly senses and intellect.

---

[7] **Vessel**. In this context, a vessel can be understood as a field of cosmic energy in the planet's magnetic sphere that brings to Earth higher laws and energies only available in distant regions of the cosmos. The term "space vessel" can also indicate vessels which may physically materialize as lights.

When one contacts subjective levels, events described in an inspired text take on a new and deeper perspective, thus that conscious part of ourselves which "studies," is able to expand. However, the Bible, or any other inspired text, tends to become outdated and eventually to be forgotten when restricted to obsolescent writings or to scientific investigation based on proven concrete facts.

Today a stalemate has set in. The truth of these documents is being investigated by means of material proof and its human authors are being sought; yet none of this should be taken into account. What matters is the Spirit which vivifies the text, the Spirit which is its origin and source.

This same childish approach considers details of the Apostle Paul's actual life and mystical experience to be an essential issue. But those facts cannot provide any clarification if one does not take into account that the Christic energy of unification and pure inclusiveness reveals itself within humans when they become open to it. If the episodes described do not become a practical possibility in the life of those who seek conscious higher evolution, they can easily lead to idolatry. Then seekers might call the apostle a saint ("Saint" Paul) and worship idols instead of becoming open to a deep transformation. As a result, the energy of the cosmic Christ in the three-dimensional world does not become the reality it could be.

Energy descends and works not only within humans but also around them in order to guide them to an inner experience. It is not meant to bring culture, theological knowledge or mystical theories, or to affiliate people in new religions or sects, which would be even more obsolete.

How can we understand the episode where Jesus walks upon the waters? How can we understand resurrection? How can we understand the fact that Lazarus walked out of his own grave? How can we understand what real virginity means? And how can we accept that servers of the Plan of Evolution have almost always had their sojourn on Earth disrupted through the violence of human beings? Intellectual answers are unsatisfactory when facts are ruled by non-material supraphysical laws which can only be understood when they are truly experienced.

When considering an inspired text one must go beyond the written word. How to do this? In The Secret Path,[8] Paul Brunton gives us some valuable hints. He suggests that we choose a book or passage to inspire us, taken from some written work that deeply appeals to the higher energies of our being, a text which helps the divine spark within our inner being to communicate with us. We should select a special paragraph and assimilate it mentally, attempting to understand all of its meanings, even the most subjective ones. In this way our mind will gradually enter a new vibration, beyond the ordinary density. If necessary, we can do this work slowly. In any case, there is no need at all to hurry, because it is not a question of getting somewhere, but rather of nurturing the more sensitive elements of our own being. Both mind and feelings must be integrated in this process without any conflict. Meanwhile, the words that we set before our consciousness vibrate within our being and open pathways. Those who dedicate themselves to this task of harmonization do not stop at isolated words; they attempt to fathom the thoughts that lie behind them. Each word should

---

[8] Paul Brunton, *The Secret Path*, [Newburyport, MA: Weiser Books], 1985.

immerge into one's consciousness and deeply imprint it, penetrating the entire subtle field of the mind. In this way, the matter which makes up the mental body gradually becomes transformed and begins to send new vibrations into deeper levels of the self.

This same instruction includes mentally repeating the chosen passage as if the reader were becoming the author (as actually happens in such cases). Taking this inspirational material as a starting point, we can build new sentences, form new paragraphs and place ourselves before them, absorbing what emanates from them as indications and as Love-Wisdom.

When we are receptive to this purifying work, we can focus on an abstract or symbolic idea so that our minds may enter other levels of perception and gradually become prepared to understand what is beyond reason. Inspired books contain values that transcend the written word, values that are to be found beneath the author's expressed thoughts. This communion produces countless experiences, such as feeling united to the source that inspired the author. When the text is elevated, its source is to be found in supraphysical dimensions and the text becomes a means to contact that source.

When we read in this way—using our inner eyes—we find passages that may become meaningful at certain moments in life. These are gifts that the inner being brings to those who seek self-purification through introspective study. It is our inner self that puts certain books into our hands. And as we acknowledge that help and open ourselves to it, we become enraptured and allow the best in us to emerge and contact our conscious world, so disrupted by the trivialities of today's civilization.

Having reached this high level and gone through this experience of unity, we should focus our attention on this inner state. Written words cease to be important. The state produced within us is then to be nurtured. In the serenity of this moment, the text can be set aside, for it has already accomplished its purpose. Its energy has penetrated us and has become sustenance for our inner world which, from then on, will convey much to us without the need for words.

To hear these inner waves and to follow their movements—such surrender prepares us for the great journey that is about to begin.

Awakening from Dense Sleep

According to some clairvoyants, the Earth emerged and developed in stages. During the first stage, the planet was not solid, but rather a mass of undulating heat and fire. It contained nothing of what we call air or the element water, only pulsating live heat.

During the second stage, a hot, gaseous element similar to air was added to the planet. A large portion of surface terrestrials will return to a similar primordial state due to the selection process currently taking place in the human species.

During the third stage, an aqueous state was added to the other states of the Earth but nothing was tangible. The tangible world came next, in the fourth stage, when the planet began to manifest typical terrestrial forms. A physical densification then took place and this is where we still live today.

Now the process is going to reverse. We will go through all those stages again, from the last to the first, until we return to the most complete abstractness. However, we will become more subtle and those stages will not appear the way they did formerly.

We are on another turn of the great evolutionary spiral, and as we experience those states, beginning with the last, they will take on new meaning and will encompass other aspects of matter.

The time has come for humankind to wake up from its dense dream and to enter less concrete levels. But not all are ready to embark on this journey. As we have seen, many human beings will be guided to another world, returning to something similar to the primordial second stage that the Earth had once experienced.

The "fire" mentioned here has nothing to do with the element that we know today. In that first stage it was something spiritual, from the sphere of the soul, not tangible at all. Contemporary human languages have no adequate word to describe it. The same applies to the descriptions of the other stages.

States of consciousness cannot be described precisely in words, especially those stages that pertain to the past or the future. Thus one must live spiritually so that one's inner being may receive and transmit the imprint of true reality to one's consciousness, without the need for any language.

Therefore it would be impossible right now to describe how the next Noah will work with the rescued humans. But we can adhere to the purest vibration we can possibly attain so that we can begin to perceive what steps we will have to take during the forthcoming transformation of the Earth.

In the same way that long ago we spoke of an "ark," today we talk about a "vessel." What was an ark, and what is a vessel? Would they be physical forms or states of consciousness? For some people, they are forms; for others, they are states. Some humans will be transported in their physical bodies as they are removed from Earth. For these, a vessel is a fairly solid structure. Others, however, will depart from the surface of the planet in their consciousness, leaving their three-dimensional bodies behind to fulfill their various destinies within the same glorious All. For them, Noah's vessel is the energy of transmigration, of transformation, of sublimation—the fulfillment of the liberation of the children of God.

The elementals, the devas and the Hierarchies that give life to fire, water, earth and air, have been fundamentally important to humans up to the present cycle on Earth. In the coming era, builders will continue working in the mineral kingdom, and especially in the plant kingdom, using even more subtle vibratory waves. In the journey back to the spiritual world and to less dense dimensions, different and more advanced Entities will be working to further human evolution. Those great Entities in charge of divine service, that help humans who leave material karma behind to enter the Law of Higher Evolution, do not deal with forms. Thus humans will relate to them differently than they do to the devas and elementals now.

Carried away by sentimentality, people have become used to creating folklore about the subtle kingdoms of Nature. Now, however, at a more mature stage, humans are less, or not at all, attracted to phenomena of the elemental and devic realms. More evolved, they have put aside their need to contact fairies, elves and flying angels, although they are aware that these builder Hierarchies will continue to take care of plants and minerals within new and still unknown energy flows. The relationship between humans and Entities of other evolutionary systems is moving toward a higher level where, for example, the cooperation of great Devas with Thaykhuma,[9] the governor of the Mirrors of the Cosmos, may be perceived.

Just as humans of the surface of the Earth raise their intellectual and mental quotients through upliftment to the spiritual and supraphysical world, the other kingdoms inhabiting the Earth also evolve. Among them, the one that has most attracted future expansions of consciousness is the plant kingdon.

As the kingdom changes consciousness, its method of contacting the elemental kingdom, the angelic kingdom and other Hierarchies also changes. In this sense, the transformation that is taking place in the building of human physical bodies is characteristic of this change. No longer will the elementals, the spirits of nature and the little devas be in charge of the formation of the fetus within the maternal womb during the process of human gestation. Physical birth will also undergo transformation.[10]

When the right time comes, we will know to what extent these Hierarchies will take care of the mineral and plant kingdoms, since humans of the surface will be engaged in some work with these kingdoms once the planet is reorganized. For instance, in the physical area of the valley of ERKS,[11] in Argentina, extraterrestrial beings and space vessels positioned on the vegetation were photographed as they worked to modify the substance or essence of certain plant species. An adaptation is also being carried out in these species so that they will be able to accompany the development of

---

[9] See Glossary.

[10] See *The Space Gardeners*, the works by Trigueirinho on page 123.

[11] ERKS is an acronym for Encontro dos Remanescentes Kosmicos Siderais—Assemblage of the Sidereal Kosmic Remainders. See Glossary.

human consciousness and thus, in the coming stage of the Earth, be able to serve people at the new level of evolution they will have attained. Extraterrestrials and intraterrestrials are also working in this delicate field of transformation.

Meanwhile, we should try to avoid being confined by old knowledge, and detach ourselves from what has already been assimilated. Let us bear in mind that knowledge is linked to evolutionary cycles and therefore becomes outdated. Humanity's helpers will be found on another level and under new conditions. In Noah's vessel, for example, fire will be seen as a new expression from the sphere of the soul or spirit rather than something that burns. We will see the same thing happen with water, which will again become a healing element on the physical level, as it was at the beginning of its materialization, likewise, with air and the earth itself. We will learn to regard all these elements in a new way.

This different way of perceiving the elements that make up this planet is part of a new state of consciousness. It is a more subtle level that humans of the surface are now going to enter. Noah is the energy that guides this evolutionary development; the vessel is the set of circumstances in which this experience takes place.

The thousands of space vessels—be they intraterrestrial, extraterrestrial, intergalactic, or intra-oceanic—which make themselves visible today, are either objects propelled in space according to laws that are unknown to us or projections of Entities and of Energies that exist in states of consciousness which are incomprehensible to the current human intellect. Some space vessels, which are materializations of the builder or rescue Hierarchies, have the initiatory powers and evolutionary force capable of helping humans to move from their current ignorant state to a more conscious one.

Even before entering the state of consciousness that we are calling "vessel" or, in biblical terms, "Noah's ark," we are able to understand that solid, liquid, gaseous, caloric or aeriform states are the externalizations of an energy that is formless in deeper reality. These forms, including the human form, are merely outer garments. Formerly we used to say that the devas created and sustained all forms. But what about today? Can we envisage other energies carrying out this work? Could not the builder Hierarchies be related to the stage of evolution the essence has attained?

The being that dwells in the human form is certainly much more integrated today than it was in the beginning of the Earth. This integration is the outcome of the synthesis of experiences lived over time, a synthesis achieved with the participation of the monad, the being's nucleus of cosmic consciousness.

Today Noah is an initiator of these issues. Let Noah tell us what we need to enter his vessel in full harmony.

Revelations for Vessel Sojourners

As the Earth experienced the successive states which we have attempted to describe in today's language, it went through a cyclical selection of beings and of species. Now, with the reversal of the order of events—as the planet goes from a solid state to a more subtle state—a new selection will take place. In olden times, such events were called a "Judgment," and since here we are talking about Noah, we will use the same term.

Forces, beings, entities or energies that fail in the Judgment enter "darkness;" those who pass it enter "light." According to spiritual wisdom, all human and physical concepts related to darkness and light are simply illusions. Light and darkness are really states. Thus, one could say that humans remain in the darkness of ignorance when they are not willing to enter the ark, whereas they enter the light of knowledge when they are willing to change their state of consciousness.

Today two groups—the beings of darkness and the beings of light—still exist side by side on planet Earth even though it has undergone various successive Judgments. At this time we are facing a new and very special Judgment. As a result, the majority of the beings of darkness will be transported to other worlds, some to planets in a steamy state, others to planets in a liquid state, similar to the Earth in ancient times. From a certain perspective, this could seem to be a step backwards, but within Evolutionary Law this "going back" to more primitive states is necessary and has its reason for existing, especially when it is understood in light of the Greater Law of Love-Wisdom.

In Love-Wisdom, each and every force, being and energy has a right to its own Dwelling Place. "My Father's house has many dwellings," said Christ when addressing the generation that heard him but understood little. Two thousands years have gone by—do we understand him today?

The rescuable humans attained their current state of light while following the path. They have always lived side by side with others who are at different points of evolution. Up until now, they have been on planet Earth together with non-rescuable beings, unable to recognize their counterparts or perceive (even when clarity was needed) who stood for light and who stood for darkness.

In Noah's ark of ancient times, terrestrial humans were not taught to make this distinction, and they were brought back to Earth without having learned anything about it, since the time had not yet arrived. But in Noah's vessel of today, all who are to be rescued will be taught this because when they return, the planet will have been totally altered. The new Earth will consciously be a planet dedicated to service. This change in the planet's state of awareness will transform everything—from the most subjective to the most objective things on its surface.

From the point of view of Noah's vessel, all the energy that rescuable beings use during their moments of external activity or during the awakened state is wasted if it is not at the service of a higher plan. As long as people continue pursuing their own interests, motivated by selfishness, they will not be able to be at ease and live peacefully within the energy of the vessel. However, rescuable beings offer all that they feel, think and do to a higher plan because they do not undergo the depletion that stems from work carried out for selfish reasons. These beings continuously receive and since they give what they receive, they go on expanding their own receptor and transmitter channels. Those who enter Noah's vessel will have been able to differentiate processes that deplete from those that create. Our life is kept vitalized if we apply our life energy towards a plan of evolution that transcends purely terrestrial activity. But if we strive merely to fulfill our own existence—and we are already aware that this kind of effort has no value within a Higher Law—we lose our life. As a result we will find ourselves in one of those states that will oblige us to retrace the steps already taken.

The minerals to be taken into Noah's vessel will not have been utilized in experiences dealing with nuclear energy or any other activity that has gradually poisoned the Earth. The plants to be taken into the vessel will not have spread toxins and in this cycle that is ending, they will have been devoted to glorifying the One Lord and to cooperating with the creator law in its most subtle aspects. The animals attracted by the beauty and the vibration of the vessel will have ceased to be carnivorous; they will have developed peaceful mental qualities and achieved feelings of love and devotion for humans. For them, people mean what "God" means to humans of the surface of the Earth.

The humans who enter Noah's vessel are those who will have attained a subtle vibration or who will have surrendered their own bodies and lives to the unknown.

Some Hierarchies in Noah's vessel are still undisclosed to terrestrials and those known to humans may presently be dedicated to new missions, since they have already fulfilled their part in the Great Plan. Humans who detach themselves from the past will enter Noah's vessel and will experience situations that are inaccessible to most people, such as not having to think about tomorrow.

"Do not concern yourselves from morning till night, and from night till morning, about what you are going to wear," said Jesus. "When you let go of apprehensiveness, when you cast off your clothing and put it under your feet, such as little children do, and step on it, then you will see the Son of the Living One and you will not be afraid."[12]

---

[12] The Apocryphal Gospel of Thomas Didymus.

New Situations for Rescued Individuals

How do the processes develop in the spiritual life inside the vessel, which, as we have seen, is a state of consciousness and at times a physical event as well? Some of the Entities present there are still unknown to humans of the surface of the Earth while others may have been perceived on the inner levels by the sojourners during their transfer.

Those who have minimized the illusions of form and who have not become caught up in the ordinary human concept of the material world will receive supraphysical vision. During their ascent into the vessel and their transfer they will not have to cross any of the regions involving emotional and mental conflicts. Everything has been prepared for this journey. If necessary, during the transfer individuals could even be encased in an extremely subtle membrane protecting them from any sort of oscillation. Engineers from Noah's immense vessel use no metal or wiring, but rather webs of energy, which the rescued individuals will get to know about at the appropriate time.

Once this subtle protective casing is removed, individuals will actually become aware of their new existence. But if they *know* beforehand that the world of forms is a world of illusions, they will almost instantly be able to perceive the reality which they will get to know more directly inside the vessel. However, it is useless to ponder how all this will come about, because the situation is completely unprecedented for the consciousness of terrestrial humans.

Each level of evolution, each level of existence, requires the work of creator, constructor or spiritual Entities having differing gradations of consciousness. Thus, as we develop, our instructors leave us (without our perceiving it) and entrust us to other instructors from the higher levels we are entering. The unity among instructors is so intrinsic that we do not even notice the change. We feel surrounded by the same kind of Love and only much later do we notice that the Being, the Energy that is helping us, is no longer the same one as before.

In preparation for the coming to Earth of Noah's great vessel, I once went to the area of the intraterrestrial city of ERKS, which, on the physical level, is located in the province of Córdoba, in Argentina. In that place filled with cosmic love, I had inner and outer contact with the energies that had been helping me ever since my arrival on the planet. There in the valley of ERKS, they all seemed to be part of a single orchestra, if such a comparison can be attributed to these benevolent beings working on Earth today, carrying out the most challenging missions. Among them there was no difference in the love they manifested.

Only beings of supreme renunciation, of total self-giving and dedication are able to carry out the task of awakening humans from their dreamland of desires, of taking them out of the illusion of three-dimensional life, and of introducing them into subtle levels of consciousness. As we know, the humans who adapted to life on the surface of planet Earth went through experimental phases of contact with the densest forces opposed to Evolutionary Energy and today they are not only caught up in chaos, but in some cases actually committed to it.

Clarity will emerge from within each person, from that inner nucleus linked to the Source of Light of the entire universe. Imbued with this truth, we can face any type of circumstance while remaining in perfect tranquility, filled with that Peace which surpasses all understanding. Noah's vessel is a symbol of that state of Peace.

◆ ◆ ◆

In the world of Noah's vessel no kind of attachment is nurtured. Noah himself, who is not the same as the Biblical one, or as the Noah from previous or future floods, carries that Love forward. Nevertheless, people who are still attached to the historical and external aspect of Noah's life and mission feel that there is only one Noah.

Yesterday's Noah is already free from being Noah. Today's Noah will be free when he has completed his current mission. There will be as many future Noahs as the evolutionary process requires. Each new level of consciousness that we attain requires us to give up what we have already acquired and the Noahs are there to help us in this process. At first they make themselves known and we begin to get used to their presence in our mind. Next they start introducing us to detachment and hence guiding us toward the vessel which is to rescue us. Finally, they receive us, helping us to adapt to new states.

The physical-etheric, astral and mental bodies have to become adjusted. The astral and mental bodies may be incorporated into one body if the individuals are to remain for some time within the vessel. Many beings will be there to help them. The Noah they knew before entering may be replaced by another. New guides may present themselves to those who have been rescued, for there has been a change in their state of awareness since they left the surface of the Earth to enter the vessel. The vessel uses resources from sub-dimensions of the physical level in order to become more concrete.

The guide that we perceive before us as we ascend to new strata of understanding always represents a higher aspect of our being. This guide stimulates us to ascend, or rather, to permit ascent to occur within us. But at the same time people can also go on seeing the Noah that they prefer. This is the reality of Cosmic Love that begins to become perceptible.

Here we can see that what really matters is Love and not so much Noah, although the figure of Noah is always cherished because it represents our inner selves which decided, come what may, to draw us out of the chaos and definitively introduce us into the great order of the universe so that we may cooperate with it.

◆ ◆ ◆

To better understand the situation of a sojourner in Noah's vessel let us take the example of a person who is asleep. To the person's inner consciousness, emotional and mental activity has fallen into oblivion and he or she has another life, as if those fluctuating bodies did not exist. The same thing happens in Noah's vessel. Those inside the vessel seem to have fallen asleep to all that happened on Earth because their distressing emotions and thoughts were given over to a dream-like state. When the physical body is transferred together with the consciousness, the brain goes through a purification process and becomes freed from memories of the Earth.

Inside the vessel people cease to be captive of earthly reasoning and they become part of something that could be called cosmic reflection. Within the vessel they are "thought" by a greater mind, and they no longer "think" the way they did on Earth. Such a state does not mean a decrease in their abilities, but rather an evolution. Ordinary thought—limited to the experiences of their human minds in the fairly distant past—gives way to a more expanded reflection and understanding as they become adjusted to the atmosphere of the vessel.

The protective energies work this way to help humans to adapt to more sublime situations. Dense emotional and mental matter is part of a more primitive state of human consciousness. Freedom is to be found in other states of consciousness, inherent to the vessel. It is impossible to attain those states with one's ordinary sensitivity. This is why, in the preparatory phases that humans go through on the surface of the Earth, they gradually learn to give up the actions, feelings and thoughts that are characteristic of the superficial states.

Inside the vessel we are well-known and we are treated with

the greatest of care. In the past, the message sent to us was much harsher, such as when Jesus said: "So, you who are in the temple, do you think that you are pure?" Jesus-Noah knows that purification has to go on being strengthened even when humans are in the vessel. The illusions of David's Pool—also cited in the apocryphal Gospel—where people used to bathe, and then dress in white but cling to the same vices and evil does not exist in the state of consciousness within the vessel.

According to Jesus, when people merely cleanse themselves superficially, "they clean the surface of the skin, such as those who perfume and adorn themselves to please men." In Noah's vessel, one's inner reality is known, and those who enter the vessel are deeply committed to a over-all purification, free to give up all identification with forms they knew on Earth.

This planet is destined to be sacred. This means that it will be freed from all lust and ready to assume its new task within the solar system. The Earth will be a wellspring of life, like the Sun, which is fully aware of being matter-spirit on all levels of manifestation. The sojourners in Noah's vessel will know how to perceive the inner side of these realities. Saint Bernard, who helped prepare for the present era, referred to the Sun as "Sun-Christ," foreseeing the awareness of that inter-relationship which is now granted to many.

The Earth today is but a shadow of what it is destined to be; it manifests no more than a mere reflection of its potential. The Earth will take on its role of Mother, as the ancient Essenes regarded Her, but without being limited to the material levels. After becoming regenerated and reordered, the Earth will continue to be a fertile field for the plant and other kingdoms to develop and will also sustain inner life without impediments for those who will dwell on its surface.

Just as Plato's morality was distinguished by its purity, the psychic atmosphere of the Earth will manifest aspects that will make its life bountiful on all levels of consciousness. People will see beyond their human hearts, which today, according to Jesus, are "full of scorpions." Their minds will no longer wield power over their incarnated self, but will become the means for humans to contact cosmic realities.

Noah is a liberator. His consciousness holds inner threads linked to the heart of each cell of rescuable humans. In his vessel, they will once and for all open their eyes to a greater reality.

In the Vessel

The humans who will be rescued into these new states still carry with them old and deep-seated traumas. In a way, their imbalances began even before the formation of the Earth, in primal worlds, in other kingdoms, where the experience of the life, which today is human, had its beginning. But these traumas were also acquired and aggravated here on the Earth, when humans chose the path of free will and consequently had to grapple with all kinds of murkiness.

Inside the vessel, Noah speaks to the right side consciousness of the rescued humans, helping all of them to understand that whatever is picked up by the senses is, in some way, the work of the Hierarchies, whose presence can be felt right there in the vessel. Some of the Hierarchies are taking care of the harmonization of the bodies while others are introducing the more awakened humans into experiences that are harmonious and of even greater significance for the being.

For the Hierarchies working in the vessel, labor is their innermost nature, so there is no possibility of dispersal. When a special need arises, the solution emerges promptly—but always from within the cosmos, from the inner life of the vessel. Humans there also understand inwardly what path they are to follow in their next stage.

The time spent in Noah's vessel is a period of clarifications and of understanding—an opportunity for the consciousness to truly take up its new position as cooperator of a greater plan. Noah helps humans to realize that even the force of the wind they knew on Earth comes from these Hierarchies, or from these Energies, that work on different levels. In this way, having made the first contacts with these realities during the time spent in the vessel, humans start to cooperate with the Hierarchies. Thus they begin to understand the winds, to become united with them, and to obtain from the winds what they need. The winds then respond to them, act in harmony with them, and cease having a merely destructive role in their lives.

Winds continue to have a destructive aspect today because humanity needs them to aid in the purification of the surface of the Earth. Desert sands will have to be carried to other areas—perhaps even to cover cities that have been contaminated. In the vessel it is known that beneath the present deserts are vast opportunities for the development of the humans who may be placed again on the surface of the Earth after having been healed and harmonized.

In the Book of Job it is written: "Behold, he holds back the waters, and they dry up; behold, he releases them and they sunder the Earth." We can see that water, as well as the wind, obey the summons. Without Noah's vessel, which is here to serve humans, those who return to live on the surface of the Earth after its reorganization according to universal laws would never be able to have that kind of direct experience.

Noah explains to the rescued humans that even the electric principle which produces lightening in the sky is the work of Beings, Entities or pure Energies. There are myriads of Hierarchies in the terrestrial sphere, and even more in the cosmos. All the possibilities, virtues and love they manifest are intrinsic to the vessel itself. Everything in the vessel is expression of the sacred.

When humans began their terrestrial life the Hierarchies created their bodies. Now the Hierarchies will receive these humans in Noah's vessel and be with them in their future cycles. As was mentioned, at each level we find new cooperators with a perfect continuity of Love-Wisdom bonding them all. When a decision is made to create a new order for beings, spiritual voices from all points of the galaxy concur and Hierarchies transmigrate to where the work is to be done.

At this moment, a profound change is being prepared in the humans of the surface of the Earth. This change will continue in Noah's vessel because many will have been removed from the Earth without having become completely attuned with, and ready for, future times.

Just as a child's consciousness has not yet unified several of its aspects, not everyone who enters the vessel will be ready to face the new times and to move on to other states of being. So, an inner work will begin with them to help them to become adjusted. In time, when they have been freed from the layers of desire and of illusion placed upon them by the Earth as part of their experience here, they will begin to perceive what they really are. In

Noah's vessel, consciousness of the personal "self" will be replaced with the consciousness of a broader "self." Individuals will come to realize that they are an essence. Their worldview and their whole way of being will then change. They will undergo a profound transformation.

The Hierarchies that help terrestrial humans also develop. However, they evolve much quicker because they have no attachments and they are already basically purified. Therefore, one should not keep on invoking a member of the Hierarchy over a length of time since that specific member may already be on another level, on another mission. All this is learned in Noah's vessel. When terrestrial humans realize this, they will probably already be somewhat aware of oneness with other beings, thus, it will make no difference to them whether this or that member of the Hierarchy is within their aura. They know that they have an inner bond with those who helped them to take the first steps, but they begin to let go of it, no matter how sublime this bond may be. Oneness becomes much more inclusive with the evolutionary ascent.

This is what happens in Noah's vessel.

Groups are also formed in the vessel. Those who already belong to an inner or spiritual group soon find out that they are part of a greater unity. Unified at all times, group members do not feel the lack of the stages they left behind and they do not bemoan their so-called "losses." In Noah's vessel there is no yearning for anything, but a bounteousness that can only be sensed by being there. Many people will soon be experiencing this.

In ordinary journeys, people do not usually let go of their earthly concerns so they become distracted from their spiritual and divine source by superfluous visions or contact with intermediary states, which do not really purify. On the other hand, during the voyage with Noah, to a great extent individuals link up with their origin, with their primal and cosmic essence.

Humans can only get to know the spiritual world when they truly aspire to live it. In Noah's vessel one lives as spirit, safely beyond the orbit of the Earth where the anticipated planetary reorganization is underway. All one's efforts to become purified and to enter the vessel are based on the recognition that spiritual sources are summoning humans to return. "Call, then, and I will answer; or I will speak and you will answer," says the cosmos in the Book of Job.

Human beings, now developed and no longer inexperienced as when they departed, will return to this subtle spiritual world.

What the Sojourners Envision

In ordinary journeys people seek externalities; however, in the vessel they enter another type of consciousness. They develop a perception that is not made up of images, but rather of content and values. At this stage, objective experiences of their lives become irrelevant. Events and actions are only meaningful at the time of choosing to enter the new state of consciousness; after that, they are useless.

Cosmic records display images, scenes and impressions from past existences, but these are not intended for the Hierarchies to pass judgment on humans, but to clarify their true state. It is no use entering the vessel without some sort of preparation. However, this does not mean schooling, but rather it is all about learning detachment, which humans were taught in every possible way during former cycles.

At the beginning of the process of purification, humans are not yet aware of their attachments. The mere fact of talking about their attachments and alleged detachments reveals how people are still subject to them. Therefore, the Hierarchies which prepare us are the epitome of patience. They always let us know that we are being accompanied and assisted but never clearly show themselves so that we do not become attached to them. We will not be able to fully recognize their loving presence until we have become fairly healed of our tendency towards attachment. If it is so difficult for ordinary humans to detach themselves from the things of Earth, what kinds of attachments would they create while still unpurified, if they were to know the things of Heaven?

♦ ♦ ♦

People's life events are not important in the vessel; what does matter is the transformation they have gone through while experiencing those events. In this way, what so far has been dreamlike imagination now evolves into direct knowledge of what really IS. This occurs in the inner world rather than in the world of changing appearances.

Considering things, events or beings as separate from one's own self is part of the earthly consciousness which rescued humans have left behind. In Noah's vessel humans regard everything as being inward and unified with themselves. In this way, service there is ongoing and sure. "There is hope for the tree that is cut for it will go on renewing itself and will not cease sprouting." This is how things are in the vessel. Everything becomes renewed.

During the first moments inside that great vessel individuals do not really perceive the spiritual entities. In the beginning their awareness is still organic, affected by residues from the mechanism developed on Earth. Little by little they begin to project themselves into the inner side of space, or rather, into the inner space of their own being. This is why, on the earthly physical level, observers have a hard time recognizing that many of the lights which appear in the sky are not really space vessels, but sheathes of beings who must make themselves visible at this time. One can only perceive reality inwardly. The external appearance of an event or of a being is merely its apparel. What must be recognized is the inner impulse that created or manifested it.

For many, Noah's vessel will probably be envisioned on the cosmic astral level, which is different from what we call the terrestrial astral level. Humanity is meant to transcend the astral level, a region of consciousness that comes immediately after the physical level and which is currently contacted by both incarnates and discarnates. However, such terms and definitions are limited by the current languages and the terminology applied by humans according to their own state of awareness and understanding. Thus it would be good to highlight that the levels of the universe are not really interposed and therefore they do not succeed one another, the way our analytical mind tends to situate them. These levels interpenetrate without being separate. They are differentiated by their very nature, not by the kind of boundaries we know from our rational education.

On the terrestrial astral level, which must now be definitively transcended, "life is more active and form is more pliant than on the physical level," explained Noah through theosophy, a spiritual philosophy which rendered much service to the planet in the past. Since astral matter is more subtle than physical matter, it easily influences humans because it pervades their earthly bodies—mental, astral and physical-etheric. Everything in humans can become very mixed up because of astral matter. This kind of heterogeneity is undesirable to those who are preparing to remain in the vessel. The state of inclusiveness, on the other hand, has nothing to do with intermixing. Inclusiveness is the state (much sought by idealists) of those who were freed from emotional residues, who rejected the instincts that are unsuitable for the more subtle evolutionary processes, and who renounced those commonplace ideas that cause people to act, feel and think the way they want to, heedless of the consequences.

Because of the instability of the forces that are almost always in conflict with one another on the terrestrial astral level, those who are in that level can easily change their appearance. This astral activity must not be confused with what takes place in the vessel when one Entity-guide is replaced by another more elevated one during the human process of evolution. From the terrestrial astral level, a negative and emotional entity, filled with the force of desire, can influence human matter. That same entity can change forms in its attempt to continue dominating peoples' feelings and actions. When repelled, it can reappear in yet another form, deceiving people and provoking countless trials.[13]

This is why, when one is inside Noah's vessel, human perception based on feelings is not valued. Today, Hierarchies take on the form of lights because in this way sojourners are only able to recognize them inwardly. Rather than something personal, this recognition is an awareness of energy of Love that rescues without influencing or dominating. Noah suggests that one should try to assimilate this information thoroughly.

◆ ◆ ◆

---

[13] Sometimes the term "entity" is applied to beings of a high evolution and sometimes to lesser forms, such as in this case. The type of entity can be identified by the meaning of the text.

What kind of awareness is present in Noah's vessel? For many it will probably be the awareness which can be created on the cosmic astral level, which differs from the terrestrial astral level. The cosmic astral level interpenetrates and elevates all the earthly states. All the levels of consciousness of this planet, from the densest physical level to what is termed "divine" level, are a preparation for the purer levels, that is, the cosmic etheric and the cosmic astral levels.

To live these experiences, which implies to distinguish whether one is encountering the earthly astral-emotional level, full of desires and illusions, or facing the pure radiation of the cosmos in its transcendent aspects, one must have a better understanding of the laws of the ether. This is possible as we gradually become receptive to these laws. Various levels of knowledge in this regard are available in Noah's vessel.

"You have everything within your reach, but you must lever your will in a spiritual sense," says the book, *The Fifth Race*.[14] "Thus, when you let yourself be guided by your inner self, you will discover the wonderful creation of which you are a part. But so far you have only admired it with the eyes of your physical body."

"The physical eye will no longer be of any use to you. You will be able to develop your own subtle garment and then, with your inner eyes, you will behold the Infinite Radiation that the Cosmos, awaiting the moment to share Its powers with all, holds for you."

This is the real festivity where nothing will be lacking.

---

[14] See *The Fifth Race*, the works by Trigueirinho on page 123.

The Virgin of Ether

During the 19th century and the beginning of the 20th, some ascended masters and elevated entities dedicated themselves to transmitting the teachings about cosmic ether and its laws, to humans of the surface of the Earth. Now, however, there is no more time for such theoretical studies, rather it is in the vessel that the "teachers" will communicate with the individuals' inner world. People will *know* that they are on another level of the ether because they will *recognize* a purer vibration. Intellectual learning will no longer predominate, as it has up to now, when masters and entities sought to adapt to this type of learning in order to reach human beings and to be understood by them.

For this reason, ascended beings such as Morya and Djwhal Khul used to express themselves through books in order to reach those who were to enter the vessel at the end of the cycle. However, in the vessel, the language has changed. These and other masters have gone on to new missions and to more subtle levels, possibly to dedicate themselves to the Earth's contact with the cosmic plane.

The earlier teachers used to explain the ether simply as the divine substance which impregnates the entire universe. In addition to that brief and concise description, there are others which can broaden our understanding of ether. For example, ether can be seen as one of the levels of the cosmos, present in Noah's vessel, which prepares humans to learn about the cosmic astral level. Ether, as universal substance, was also intended to be conveyed through the image of the Virgin Mother, present in many world religions. However, because those religions increasingly abandoned their more subtle principles in order to focus on material matters, this ancient image was distorted and transformed into a cult of personages, albeit pure ones. The Virgin Mother is not really a person, but rather the very heart which issues Matter, Life, Force and Action, both known and unknown to human beings. Although some celestial beings in their earthly sojourn *represented* this state, none could have ever *been* the Cosmic Virgin Mother as such, no matter how elevated their spiritual state. Not being a physical entity, the Cosmic Virgin in all plenitude could never be limited to form, to an earthly vehicle. Whoever studies *Mother's Agenda*[15] will see clearly that perfection does not exist on the physical level.

In Noah's vessel, the human mindset undergoes a profound conversion. Face to face with Noah, a pure and universal being, individuals can see that they must consider him not only as a "higher" being, but also as an elder and more experienced brother. This helps earthly humans to become liberated and to reduce their

---

[15] *Mother's Agenda* [Chambly, Quebec:Institute de Recherches Evolutives, Canada] 1988.

idiosyncrasies.

Nevertheless, this ether is not what we call astral light; it is a material phenomenon, but more subtle than what is known in the material world. The Virgin Mother is far above all phenomena. Cosmic ether is also not the kind of ether known to current earthly science; it is a material substance that is so subtle it cannot be measured by instruments. Cosmic ether is a spiritual conduit that can transmit to humans, states of consciousness that would otherwise be inaccessible to them. The aid of the Virgin Mother is an omnipresent reality that does not depend on cults or ritualism. Nor does it depend on fanatic manifestations, for on the cosmic level and in Noah's vessel, nothing could be denser than fanaticism. Noah's vessel represents one of the vehicles needed to eventually attain this higher consciousness.

The itinerary of the vessel journey is made up of a series of renunciations made with joy. This is so because at this point of the process humans already understand that each object and each person released will mean greater freedom both for themselves and for the other. The sojourners in Noah's vessel will have understood this and will be ready to take up those liberating deeds.

For those who will not journey in Noah's vessel, all this will seem like mere repugnant ideas or nothing but suppositions. Future fellow sojourners will be able to recognize one another by their sensitivity towards the principles of the vessel and by the ease with which they adapt to suraphysical realities that can only be validated inwardly.

Whenever one penetrates celestial ideas or attains subtle understanding, one comes upon the Akasha, the most concrete synthesis of the cosmic ether. Cosmic ideas are imprinted in the Akashic Record where human channelers can *read* what will later be transformed into messages that make up the *sacred books* of the world. The books belong to the world, but the ideas attempted to be expressed in them come from the Akasha. In order to reproduce these ideas for others, those who have direct contact with them cannot avoid intermixing the ideas with some of their own impressions. This is why the great teachers of humanity, who were liberators and not slaveholders, warned that sacred books should be considered only as a support. Once the first impulse was given by those instructive and instrumental texts, it was up to humans to create their divine environment within themselves and avoid getting crystallized in the obsolescence of the texts themselves.

In the Apocryphal Gospels an episode describes five year-old Jesus together with other children, molding clay birds. The Law of Moses forbade any type of work on that day, the Sabbath. An adult saw them and went to complain to the boy's father. Joseph went to the place where the children were and questioned Jesus: "Why are you doing what is not allowed on a Sabbath?" Without answering, Jesus looked at the twelve clay birds he had shaped and said to them: "Fly!" The clay birds came to life, spread their wings and took flight, chirping loudly.

◆ ◆ ◆

Great was the devastation on the surface of the Earth caused by crystallized understanding of texts that were originally given as inspiration! Wars, struggles and divisions were instigated because the obsolete external form of these texts no longer corresponded to the new movements of energy. Thus, humans went so far as to kill in the name of God, despite the basic mandate expressed in certain sacred books—*do not kill*. Ignorance gradually prevailed because the human intellect was not able to conceive unforeseen situations such as those generated by spiritual reality.

However, this phase is coming to an end and the vessel of today's Noah will now receive all those who are ready to be definitely freed from stagnation. As for the others, the same Law of Love will direct them by diverse streams of energy and forces toward levels compatible with their state. The saying: "My Father's house has many dwellings." is valid as much for those who are ascending as for those who are descending the path. The Law of Evolution is present in both instances, only its secondary aspects vary. In some worlds the Law of Evolution allows material karma to operate forcefully; in others it permits karma to be more diluted by Cosmic Love; and in still other worlds this Law manifests higher and more liberating aspects.

The Apocryphal Gospels tell of another occasion when the child Jesus went out to the fields with his father during the sowing season. Joseph was planting wheat and Jesus took a grain and threw it on to the earth. Later on, when the grain harvested from that place was milled, it produced huge amounts of flour. All the poor of the area were called in and even after receiving abundantly, there was still plenty left over.

Could not this episode be a foretelling of the new and expanded states that await us?

Letting Go of the Guardians

Whoever begins to see images or hear voices and sounds when starting the inward process would do well to mistrust such manifestations and even reject them. To cooperate with purification one must detach oneself from everything that is perceptible. "Who will draw what is pure from what is soiled" asks the Book of Job. "Nobody," comes the answer. But in Noah's vessel the way is open before us. Those who were brought into the vessel are already aware that they are light and that they were made for the light—therefore they hold themselves apart from what the outer or inner senses still show them.

The outer senses were shaped according to the influence of the environments on the development of the three-dimensional part of humans which was to live on Earth. So the ability of these senses to perceive is superficial. The organs of the human body were formed to serve outer awareness; consequently they are of little use inside Noah's vessel, where everything is perceived from within. These organs therefore have to be transformed and endowed with the ability to function inwardly.

Even before the journey begins, highly evolved micro-organs are implanted in the physical organs of the rescuable humans and a gradual transformation takes place. This task is completed in Noah's vessel, which is also a great laboratory. The same type of assistance will be given to plants for them to evolve rapidly before they are taken back to the surface of the planet at the end of the great purification. Minerals and animals will also be assisted, and through the Law of Compensation the millennia dissipated by humans through exploitation of these kingdoms of Nature will be recovered.

Once they are transformed the senses will make it possible for humans to perceive the inner world. As a result they will be able to get to know their true state as Monads. Those who know that the Monad has a very subtle body will be given the opportunity to perfect their inner perceptions to the maximum. Pure formless Entities and Energies will only gradually be manifested to humans. Only when individuals cease to nurture expectations, will these forms be completely abandoned. The process of evolution is subtly educational; by means of this process all concepts regarding the teachings that were created in the three-dimensional world, will fall away. In Noah's vessel education is not transmission of theoretical and formal knowledge, but rather support and stimulation of the inner being so that through its innermost experience it may draw closer to ever-deeper realities.

When those who are taken into the vessel become aware of their inner reality, they will be ready to receive tasks, to serve and later—if it is their path—to be transferred back to Earth. This is all guided by Hierarchies of wise ones who have already been through the human stage, in previous eras of the Earth or on some other planet. These wise ones have therefore been liberated from all attraction to dense matter and they know well the process by which humans become more subtle.

Just as the exodus of biblical history was necessary in the past, today humans must withdraw into Noah's vessel in order to resolve their ambivalences. Ambivalence belongs to the Earth and by surmounting it all human nature becomes transformed. Rescued humans must indeed be kept temporarily within the core of the vessel so that they may let go of their tendency toward ambivalence. Hence, in the future, they may be able to experience unity in their life on the physical level.

In the past, in order to populate the Earth, humanity had to become progressively denser. To inhabit the Earth after the great purification, human consciousness and bodies will need to become more subtle. Once people have attained a certain link with the subtle worlds and are able to perceive the inner self of other beings (and so be able to really help others) they will no longer be so dense. They will be capable of participating in the life of the stars, which will be able to manifest themselves no longer as mere points of light in the sky, but as the path humans are to consciously follow toward the infinite.

Each stage of development follows laws that pertain to it. Humanity will gradually be able to incorporate the new laws into its consciousness as it fulfills the laws already known. Most humans are still far away from these realities because they have not even managed to obey the Ten Commandments given at the beginning of this civilization, which is now facing Judgment. The Ten Commandments were clear but they were not followed. Instead of fulfilling them, people sought theological expressions to justify their own negligence—their habitual surrendering to dense matter and to the psychological mechanism that was given to them as a test.

In remote eras, humans remained in a non-physical state until the Earth was ready to receive them. Now, in different states, humans will also await the reorganization of the Earth. Forces of involution will no longer manipulate their destiny. After this test of exercising free will, the few who have freed themselves from this mental state of uncertainty will not revert to being dense the way they were. Humans, as well as beings from the other kingdoms, will gradually take on forms appropriate for their evolutionary needs. For this to happen, millions of vessels are present in the environs of this planet. The largest of these is Noah's vessel and Noah is the supreme commander. Since the beginning, Noah has dedicated himself to accompanying the beings who will definitively leave this great earthly adventure, as well as those who will return to the Earth to participate in its new life under new laws.

Nonetheless, let us prepare to let go of this great guardian so that we may be able to recognize the next stages we are to live and to release him to follow his ascending cosmic destiny. Let us not repeat what we did when he was incarnated as Jesus. Let us not worship his person, thus neglecting to really follow him. Let us remember that to *follow him* does not mean to cling to him, but rather to fulfill the Law given by him so that we can ascend to the infinite, with him and with those faithful to what they learn. Let us remember that to *follow him* does not mean to fight for him, but rather to tread in his footsteps, which are usually very different from the footsteps of those who allege to be his representatives and consider themselves to be entrusted with his teachings.

◆ ◆ ◆

Noah tells us that two thousand years ago, Jesus was rightly called Christ, but since then Jesus also has evolved. Religions and sects of the world insist on affirming that Jesus has always been perfect because they do not want to let go of the convenience of using this immobility to endorse their temporal institutions, which retain castes at the expense of the work and ignorance of others. Within the Cosmic Law of Evolution no being is ever deprived of the right to evolve. Therefore, Jesus will always go on evolving.

During the incarnation where he was assigned to embody the Christ Entity, Jesus went through an intense process of ascent. As an Essene, he was a messenger of the Great Fraternity which brought yet unknown divine teachings to humans. Blavatsky says that Jesus always lived a life of exemplary purity. This is the basic condition for someone to become a teacher of humans. Compassion and love for humanity must be explicit, not in words, but in actions and in a life that abides by higher laws as well as earthly ones.

According to history, Jesus raised the dead and healed the sick; he even made the crippled walk and the blind see. Few people were able to perform such wonders as he, not even those who wielded black magic. When thaumaturgists work with healing, they do not really remove the ills but simply dislocate them temporarily. With Jesus, liberation was forever because before he performed the "miracle," he saw the person's inner willingness to unite his or her own individual will with Cosmic Law. From then on, there would not be enough time for imbalance to set in. To recognize this inner condition and then to mediate the healing was one of Jesus' tasks on Earth during that incarnation, which has been universally acknowledged.

Jesus manifested the prominent aspect of the cosmic Energy of Love-Wisdom and this prompted him to express sublime laws during his conversations along the byways, in the fields, on the hillsides bordering the lakeshores. There was no special place he had to be in order to transmit his teaching. Churches were founded only after he disincarnated. In the midst of crowds, he taught in the open air or wherever he was. From among what he left for us to study, some laws were kept more veiled and not revealed to everyone. Those who received this teaching handed it down as well as they could, according to their own responsibility. We do not criticize any of them, for this would be incompatible with the energy of Noah's vessel.

All the teachers of humanity demonstrated the wisdom of *knowing* when to talk and when not to talk about something. This calls for self-control, which Jesus clearly expressed. Even his way of walking, according to history, revealed poise and deep assurance. For people who needed proof, his steadfastness, even when facing "death" and physical suffering, confirmed the authenticity of what he preached because he lived what he taught.

Those who became attached to the magnificent manifestation in Jesus that occurred two thousand years ago failed to perceive a more recent, and in some aspects, an even stronger, manifestation in the human physical form of Apollonius of Tyana. Banned from history by the Christian Church because he possessed characteristics similar to those of Jesus and also expressed them even more clearly, Apollonius of Tyana was the reincarnation of Jesus after his crucifixion and ascension.

Blavatsky—a beacon whom Noah holds close to his heart—did not reveal that Apollonius of Tyana was a reincarnation of the man Jesus, although she did present him as an admirable philosopher who appeared in Cappadocia at the beginning of the first century of the Christian era. He studied the science and philosophy of his times, and only later became a teacher. During his hundred and five years of physical life he ate only fruit and vegetables. He never drank any wine, which, for some "followers" of Jesus, was a real heresy. Those who followed the external image of the Being did not perceive that they were clinging to a form while failing to see Apollonius as perfecting this form within the higher Law of Evolution.

According to theosophical revelation, Apollonius had achieved a notable subtleness of physical matter. His garments were only of plant fibers, he walked barefoot and his hair reached down to his feet—a question of magnetic balance with which he was thoroughly familiar. By mentioning the external features of Apollonius we do not intend readers to imitate these traits physically, but rather to become predisposed to seek conscious, inner contact. People still get impressed with appearances but attempting to replicate the characteristics of another on the physical level causes individuals to become separated from one another. As we know, living conditions today are different and life priorities are not always manifested externally.

Under the physical aspects of Jesus, this Being received initiations before he was thirty years old and went to meet the masters of the Himalayas, Tibet and Egypt. While manifesting the physical features of Apollonius of Tyana, he received more advanced initiations in the Temples of Aesculapius, in Greece. In this way, through new expansions of consciousness, the energy sheathed in the form of Apollonius performed even greater and more subtle miracles than it did as Master Jesus. He also practiced cosmic healing, thus he was able to be an invaluable channel for the fathers of medicine, called "gods" by the Greeks of those times. Jesus himself had already affirmed: "In truth I tell you: whoever believes in me will also do the works that I do, and even greater works than these." (John 14:12)

Apollonius prepared himself for a higher initiation by keeping external silence for five years, never uttering a word, and by journeying to find those with whom he had an affinity and staying with them in Antioch, in Ephesus, in Pamphylia and in other regions. Apollonius also went to India. India represented the energy that was developing on Earth at that time, that is, the planetary masculine polarity. In Babylon, Apollonius was initiated into other mysteries, with the help of Chaldeans who introduced him into the art of prophecy. He was thus able to foretell events that later took place on the physical level, such as earthquakes, the deaths of royalties and other significant events of those times.

The human biases experienced in his previous incarnation as Jesus were repeated with Apollonius and once again he was rejected by the priests. In Lesbos they felt threatened by the power of Apollonius who set humans free instead of prevailing over them. The priests of Orpheus at first tried to withhold his access to certain mysteries. Admittedly, these mysteries were then revealed to him by means that the Evolutionary Law always uses when needed. If the development of humanity depended on the earthly wise ones, we would all be worshiping beings that were committed in some way to obsolete practices. But development is the work of the cosmos and the cosmos is always present, even in such dismal situations as the self-destructing conditions brought about daily by the present civilization of the surface of the planet.

Like Jesus, Apollonius could control the laws that govern hurricanes, seaquakes, earthquakes and the fiercest wild animals. However, there was evidence that this Being had progressed since his manifestation as Jesus. Apollonius was able to have direct and effective influence on the great leaders of his times inducing kings and queens to change the course of many decisions. At the end of his incarnation he began to work with a few selected disciples. However, unlike the disciples of Jesus, who betrayed him more than once, these disciples were liberated from the possibility of betraying him.

◆ ◆ ◆

In the state of consciousness of Noah's vessel there is no intention of creating any cult of Apollonius of Tyana. In fact, the energy present in Jesus, and right after that, in Apollonius, manifested other times in a more subtle form. Today that energy is represented by Samana, a cosmic name that indicates its new level of vibration. Samana no longer walks this Earth, raising the dead and healing the sick. This energy now works on another level, drawing together all those who are committed to a higher evolutionary life. Not only has the work of the energy expanded with Samana, it has also actuated the work outlined by Jesus two thousand years ago. Jesus affirmed that he would be with us until the end of these times and, as the manifestation of Samana, he, the Noah of today, is truly here.

After the time spent in Noah's vessel, some people will be put back on the surface of the Earth where they will find new laws and a supra-nature that is more refined and even wiser than the nature that is here today. Others will transmigrate to different planets in this or in other solar systems, for example, more evolved individuals who may have attained a certain level of consciousness in non-material evolution and are apt to go beyond the earthly human race. Individuals are usually transmigrated in consciousness and not in their dense bodies, unless they are to go to planets governed by laws similar to those of the Earth where physical human life of the surface is being developed.

In the past the Moon had to become detached from the Earth to allow for certain conditions of development here. Now the forces of involution have to be driven out of planetary environs so that a new development may take place through higher laws of evolution. To eject these forces is not a human task, thus in Noah's vessel no mention is made of them. On the other hand, it is up to humans to dissolve the heterogeneity that currently exists among peoples.

In the very beginning, the human forms that were developed on the Earth's primitive continents were relatively empty. Gradually souls coming from different planets, some more evolved than others, began to inhabit those bodies. This descent went on until the time of Atlantis, producing a great variety of beings who thus made up the race of the surface of the Earth. The very different origins of the souls gave rise to the heterogeneous and disunited humanity of today. Psychology is still unable to detect the origin of a soul and consequently cannot treat it correctly. But this science is also under the Law of Purification. In the vessel and through Noah's work, Psychology will be transformed into a mode of perception still unknown to us.

Changes are also being prepared on the physical level of the Earth, and in Noah's vessel the bodies of rescued individuals are being adapted accordingly. Just as today's soil and atmosphere are different from those at the time of Atlantis[16] (where the air breathed was permeated with mist and steam), in the future, weather conditions, atmospheric pressure, and the rays of the sun will also be different. The new habitat will help humans become more subtle. Water will become radioactive and healing, as before. The plant kingdom will provide humans with increasingly refined vegetables, fruits and grains. All of these conditions will facilitate the development of the nucleus of light that is present within each cell of the physical body.

Just as the mists of Atlantis dispersed, today's illusions and desires will also become dissolved so that earthly conditions may allow for the development of spirit, of its laws and of its most sublime plans. The individuals being prepared in Noah's vessel will be ready to live according to what was proclaimed:

"Seek to augment what is small and diminish what is large. Thus, when you enter a house and ask for food, do not consider yourselves worthy of taking the high places at the table; do not even go near them so that the host will not have to say to you: 'Sit

---

[16] See Glossary.

lower,' and thus mortify you. But if you go to the lower places at the table, with those who are less than you, the host will say to you: 'Come higher up,' and this will be good for you."

And the Apocrypha continue: "If you have not been faithful in small things, what will happen to you in the large ones?"

Samana and Other Noahs

In Noah's vessel one learns to see past-present-future as a single image. In this way, long cycles of human history are portrayed as a summary, which makes it almost impossible for the mind that is adapted to a three-dimensional world to distinguish one cycle from another. This great vessel will be commanded by Samana, also known cosmically as Sananda. During the time when he walked the Earth and manifested himself to humanity as Jesus, this Being said that he would remain with us until the last day, when he would come to get his "flock." As Noah, his vessel will carry out the rescue envisioned for the end of this cycle. "Hounds and sorcerers, prostitutors, murderers, idolaters, those who love to lie and deceive, will all be left behind." These words, uttered on the Island of Patmos at the beginning of the Christian era, continue resounding until today.

◆ ◆ ◆

"Blessed are they who read and who hear the words of this prophecy and abide by what is written therein; for the time is near."

"Behold, he will suddenly come with the clouds, and every eye will see him, even the eyes of those who pierced him."

"For as in the days of the flood, they ate, drank and got married, until Noah entered the ark. And they knew nothing until the deluge swept them away."

"And so it will be with the coming of the Son of man."

"It will be like in the days of Lot, when they all ate and drank, sold and planted and built until Lot left Sodom. And then fire poured down from the sky."

"Those who are in Judea, flee to the hills; those who are on the streets, do not go into your homes; those who are in the field, do not go back to get your clothes."

"Remember Lot's wife."

◆ ◆ ◆

There will be different forms of rescue. Some individuals will walk to specific locations which will be indicated beforehand or when the time comes. Others will be fetched wherever they are. Since Noah's vessel is immense and would not be able to approach the surface of the Earth, it will remain in the upper strata of the atmosphere. All operations will be carried out by smaller space vessels that come down from it. They will project a sort of energy cone which will draw and rescue those who are ready for the higher Law of Evolution and take them right away to the large space vessel.

The smaller space vessels may also land and, after adapting their magnetic field to that of human beings, they will allow people to enter tranquilly.

"Two will be in the field: one will be taken and the other left behind."

"Two will be at the mill: one will be taken and the other left behind."

"Two will be in bed: one will be taken and the other left behind."

"Be prepared, for you do not know the hour in which the Son of man will come."

Some people ask: why do so few know of these things? Noah says: "When I speak to you, I am speaking to everyone. Blessed are they who are doing their duty when the Lord comes."

In the vessel, the astral-emotional and mental bodies of rescued individuals will not disintegrate but will first undergo harmonization and then merge, becoming one body. This is why it has been said that "those who triumph will not undergo the affliction of the second death," meaning the "astral death"[17] experienced by ordinary humans who will not enter the vessel. "I will give you the crown of life."

"I know of your works; behold, I have put an open door before you and no one can close it." In Noah's space vessel this open door is the *right side consciousness*, the possibility for people to have direct knowledge and to receive all the guidance needed for their evolution.

"Here I am at the door and knock; if somebody hears my voice and opens the door, I will enter the home and will dine with

---

[17] See Glossary.

him, and he with me." This is not only a promise, but also a state of enduring union that is to be recognized, a presence to be perceived even before the expected events become visible. "I come without delay."

Therefore, to those who ask when this will take place, one can say that it is already happening, and that it could be perceived if one were not using only the physical senses. "But the evil ones will say in their hearts: 'My lord is delaying.' And they will gather round their servants and they will eat and drink with drunkards, and the lord will come unexpectedly."

◆ ◆ ◆

"But when you see rebellions and hear talk of wars, do not be disturbed. For that will come before the end."

"Nations will fight against nations, kingdoms against kingdoms, and there will be great signs and shocks. Then they will hate you and kill you. But not a single hair of your head will perish."

Noah's energy, which has always been only one, speaking through Jesus, said that humans would be granted to "sit upon the throne."

"Just as I triumphed," said the Jesus of those times, "and I sat with my Father on his throne, I will also grant those who triumph to sit with me."

According to the patterns of behavior that future humanity will live, the terms *right side consciousness* and *left side consciousness* refer mainly to consciousness and not only to the hemispheres of the brain. The sides of the physical body correspond to states of consciousness that exist according to people's *inner attitude*. *Right* signifies openness to abstract levels which encompass archetypal ideas and the plan of evolution. *Left* means openness to concrete facts, stratified social and cultural concepts, and trivial ideas, such as profit and other typical notions of the commonplace way of life.

It is not possible for us to foresee what the life of the rescued will be like inside the vessel, for they will be increasingly attuned with the *right side consciousness*. The awakening which all will experience during the process of becoming attuned with higher levels, by Law will draw them towards ever broader and more universal service, ultimately leading them to give up their egoistic lives.

◆ ◆ ◆

As we know, the opportunity given to humanity today has its roots in ancient times.

In those days, giants inhabited the Earth. They began to procreate and bear daughters. Men saw that those women were beautiful and took them for themselves. These women gave birth to the so-called "dauntless" humans known in ancient times and evil set into the Earth. Then the Creator Lord regretted having placed humans in the world and said: "I will cast off the face of the Earth those humans which I created, all, from man to animal, to the reptile and the bird in the air, because I repent having made them."[18]

At that time Noah, a just and righteous man, evolved consciously and walked with God on this corrupt and violent Earth.

---

[18] See the Bible, Book of Genesis.

God spoke to Noah: "The end of all flesh has come before my face for the Earth is full of violence and so I will wipe them off the Earth." He then told Noah to make a wooden ark, with many compartments, covering both the inside and the outside with tar. He told him to make a window in this ark and a door next to it. According to instructions, the ark would have floors to accommodate different levels of beings.

"And behold, I will bring forth a great flood of waters upon the Earth," God told Noah, "to undo all flesh." Furthermore: "All that is on Earth will perish. But with you I will establish my covenant: you will enter the ark together with your sons, and with your wife, and with the wives of your sons. And of all that lives, of all flesh, two of each species will you place in the ark, to keep them alive with you and these are to be male and female."

Just as today, in those times almost nobody believed this would happen. But God continued speaking to Noah: "Two of each species will come to you, so that you may keep them alive. And take for yourself all kinds of edible food and keep it with you and this will serve for your and their sustenance." So Noah did what God had instructed. Then he was told to enter the ark, since the time had come.

And Noah and his sons and his wife and the wives of his sons went into the ark because of the waters of the deluge. From all flesh that had spirit and life, two by two they entered Noah's ark. And the Lord closed it from outside. And in the second month, on the seventeenth day of the month, all the springs of the great abyss burst open and the windows of the sky were opened. And for forty days and forty nights there was rain on Earth so that all that had been created should be wiped out.

◆ ◆ ◆

The waters of the deluge rose, lifting up the ark, and all the high hills under the sky were covered. All the flesh that remained outside the ark perished, including the birds and the cattle and the beasts, the reptiles that crawl upon the earth and the humans with benumbed consciousness. And thus all substance on the face of the Earth was undone, except Noah and those with him.

The waters covered the Earth for one hundred and fifty days, until God sent a wind that made them go down. The springs of the abyss and the windows of the sky were closed and the rain stopped. The waters gradually went down and in the seventh month the ark came to rest on the mountains of Ararat.

The waters receded until the tenth month when the peaks of the mountains reappeared. Noah opened the window and let out a crow, which went back and forth without finding dry soil. He then let out a dove, to see if the waters had gone down. The dove did not find where to rest because the waters were still covering the face of the Earth. It returned to Noah who then took it and put it back into the ark.

Noah waited another seven days and again sent out the dove. This time it returned when it was already late, carrying an olive twig with green leaves in its beak. Noah understood that a new stage had arrived. He waited for seven more days and again sent out the dove, which did not come back. Noah took the cover off the ark, looked outside and saw that the earth was dry.

God then said to him: "Leave the ark, you and your wife, and your sons and their wives. Bring out with you all the animals that are with you, of all kinds of flesh, of bird, of cattle, of all reptiles that crawl on the Earth, and populate the Earth abundantly and be fruitful."

And God continued speaking to him, telling him what we need to hear today: "Never again will I curse the Earth because of humans, for the imagination of the human heart has been evil since childhood." And he blessed Noah and his children, telling them to develop and increase their gifts and potentials. "All that moves and is alive," he continued, "will be for your sustenance; I have given you all kinds of green herbs. But flesh, with its life, which is to say, its blood, you shall not eat."

In the course of time these directives were forgotten. But, in those days God affirmed: "Whoever spills the blood of men, by men will his blood be spilled; because God made man according to his image."

◆ ◆ ◆

There have been many Noahs, not only this one. They are mentioned in the Bible, but it is not made clear if they are the same one or others. There are also various Noahs today. The greatest of them all announced thousands of years ago that he would be with us until the end of time. And where is he now? In some geographical area? In some place on the physical level? Would his ark be made of tarred wood, such as the one described in the Bible? Or could it be a vehicle capable of shifting dimensions, of transferring from one level to another, of moving at a speed infinitely faster than light, and of going inward, as pure consciousness? The sojourners will get to know all of this.

In an epistle, Peter speaks about the day of rescue: "The day of the Lord will come like a thief, where the skies will fall with a great rumble, and the elements, aflame, will fall apart and the Earth and all works thereon will burn." And he goes on: "All things having thus to perish, what type of person is it advisable for you to be in holy conduct and piety?" As we await this moment, we should, according to Peter, be "immaculate and irreproachable in peace."

"Grow in grace and in knowledge," for "few things of the world serve for the one necessary thing," proclaims the vessel in another part of its teachings expressed in an apocryphal Gospel.

The Muslim oral records attribute to Jesus the following apocryphal warning: "Love of this world and love of the future cannot remain together in the heart of one who believes, just as water and fire cannot remain together in the same container."

"Whoever seeks the world," it continues, "is like someone who drinks sea water. The more he drinks, the thirstier he gets until the water kills him." Sea water here represents desire, which is endless and increases the more it is quenched. People of this civilization are far from perceiving this reality. The same force that feeds retrograde social and economic structures teaches and conditions people to develop desire, universally represented by excessive consumption of material goods, which they insist on calling progress.

Thus, many are the lamps "that the wind blows out." And

many are the called whom "vanity corrupts." But "happy are those who discard the momentary passion for a future good they have not yet seen."

SECOND PART

Those Who Do Not Listen

The same thing is happening today as in the past when almost nobody believed what was to come.

A teacher who came to the Earth has given us the following overview:[19] "Where so many creatures are at early stages of the descent into ego-experience and ego-development, it is foolish to expect them to respond to teachings suitable for advanced stages alone—where the need is for growing release from the ego. The first group naturally and inevitably has different, even opposing, outlooks, trends, ideas, beliefs, inclinations, and desires from those of the second one. It wants to enlarge the ego, whereas the other wants to diminish it. To condemn it as wrongly directed is ignorant, impractical, and mistaken. If the history of mankind has teemed with war and bloodshed in the past, part of the cause can be found here. But that same history moves also in cycles. We stand today between two cycles, two eras, two cultures. The next one will not only be new, it will also be brighter and better in every way."

---

[19] Paul Brunton, *Perspectives— The Timeless Way of Wisdom*, p.155,161 [Burdett, New York: Larson Publications, 1984].

This teacher of modern times stated: "Powerful forces in the heaven worlds are gathering for a transmission and will enter our world at an appropriate time, which is fixed and measurable within this century. These forces will stimulate new thoughts and new feelings, new intuitions and new ideals of a religious, mystical, and philosophic kind in humanity. It will verily be the opening of a new epoch on earth..."

All of this is Noah's vessel, seen from another point of view and declared by the mentalist philosopher, Paul Brunton, who stated that to arrive at a great certitude is to arrive at great strength. Truth not only clears the mind but also arms the will; it is not only a light to our feet but is itself a force in the blood.

So let us first recognize the truth, in order to free ourselves from all present-day fetishes and to open our consciousness for the great journey. Paul Brunton heartens us affirming that deep down within the heart there is stillness which is healing, a trust in the universal laws which is unwavering, and a strength which is rock-like. But because it is so deep we need both patience and perseverance when digging for it.

This is the time to count on that strength and to prepare ourselves to recognize the vessel and the meeting place.

◆ ◆ ◆

The planet we inhabit is still divided into territories demarcated by clear-cut boundaries. Two great and prosperous countries once received and accepted tasks that were to be carried out for the good of all.

One country had the worldwide mission to help those who were weaker; therefore it would have to develop the resources needed for its own people and also aid the underprivileged in every way.

The other country, even larger in territory, was to take up the task to unite nations and it was permitted to begin this task by congregating them into one political unit.

The first could not resist the consumption of superfluous goods, and consequently became engrossed in its own economic and material enrichment. The second allowed itself to be carried away by the gratification of domination and power and chose to submit the others to its utilitarian ideas.

Both countries failed in their initial proposals which had been inspired by the more universal levels of planetary consciousness. As a result, two other countries with an ancient tradition of waging war began to organize a sort of axis of collusive forces. One of them brought down the wall that had divided it in a postwar partitioning. The other took advantage of the failure of the first two countries that had evolutionary and spiritual functions and began re-establishing world dominion, this time, however, through the economy.

In this way, the axis of forces of involution (the same as in the 1940-1945 war), was rebuilt, and a cycle of life on planet Earth began to come to a close. Since then, we have been witnessing the final confrontation between the forces of involution and the positive energies, these latter being represented by isolated individuals rather than by any nation. The difference is that, at this stage, those positive individuals work more inwardly, while the representatives of the forces of involution will take over the external scene and destroy one another, as we will see.

◆ ◆ ◆

It is understandable that the two countries have failed in their efforts and moral commitment to the rest of the world (which thus learned not to expect salvation from anything external). One need only know their history, full of crimes and transgressions of Higher Laws, to have a prophetic picture of their future.

Throughout the stages of development of these two countries one can see that progress was built on crimes and suffering—from their "discovery," through what is historically called the period of "exploration and conquest," then through the stage of founding cities, establishing colonies, and the inevitable wars of territorial expansion, moving on through their internecine revolutions, the massacre of indigenous peoples and commercial exploitation of neighboring or distant countries, and finally reaching the stage of research and use of nuclear energy.

In some historic photos of those discordant events, one can see individuals who had been born to bring peace, meeting to declare war. Sidereal space exploration became the object of conquest, when in reality space belongs to all. One can see, then, how immaturity can cause humans and nations to yield to the influence of forces of involution. They enter space without knowing the laws of balance and harmony; they send out probes and solid objects that pollute, destabilize and violently perforate the ether, and, within the law of cause and effect, bring terrible destruction to the planet.

The imbalance of the Earth's surface has reached a point of

no return, beyond the control of today's science. The basis of the universe is equilibrium, which guarantees that planets and other stars subsist in harmony and do not collide in space. Meanwhile humans plunder, exploit and deplete natural resources in the name of so-called progress and to benefit their own lifestyle. Among the results of so many crimes, the seas, such as the Aral Sea in Central Asia, are turning into deserts (the wind annually covers each acre with almost a quarter of a ton of sand and salt), ocean life is perishing, especially the North Sea in Europe, and the arable surface of the Earth is becoming sterile and poisoned.

◆ ◆ ◆

Signs of the ending of a cycle are here.

The media have disclosed that air and water contaminated by the use of toxic chemicals in agriculture are causing diverse genetic anomalies. Scientists admit that the situation is worsening, while efforts to preserve the natural surroundings continue to be fruitless.

Water is already becoming scarce in many parts of the planet and the threat to humanity's survival becomes more hazardous day by day. Scientists believe that, if necessary, seawater could be made potable by removing the salt. Such a procedure would be an aggression to the human etheric and astral body, for no technology known on Earth today can eliminate the toxic elements that the seawater has absorbed in the subtle levels.

The number of children born with congenital malformations is increasing, and in various regions of the Earth women living near nuclear power plants are recommended not to breastfeed babies due to the risk of their milk being contaminated. Although statistics are not always precise, the signs are clear that the time has come to "close" the door of the vessel.

In the nineteen eighties a Pope had already declared publicly: "Humanity is on the path of destruction." This is even more evident today. Within the material laws that we know, no process of deliverance and balance is possible. The increase of assassinations and of civil and military violence suggests to those who are more aware that the time has come to seek contact with the supraphysical levels, with Noah's vessel, where the solutions are to be found.

Communication with these supramental levels can occur, not because human thought is omnipotent, but because, according to Noah's instructions, universal thought encompasses space. Only the reckless believe in miracles. Miracles are no more than unusual events which science and humans of the Earth do not yet understand. In his writings, Paul Brunton has explained that both powers and phenomena may appear miraculous, but they really come about through occult laws that are inherent to peoples' very being, for just as human consciousness is capable of manifesting powers that contradict psychological knowledge, the human body is capable of manifesting phenomena that contradict medical knowledge.

We must hold this pure philosophy of Noah's vessel in our consciousness, for nothing that exists in the three-dimensional world can solve the human problems on Earth at this time. Up until now, the learned have been given all the signs they needed. The time has come to seek inner silence so that the call may be heard and guidance for the next step may be perceived.

Other Floods

One day people received the following information from the news media: "The clocks are going to be put back one second on the 31st" because all timepieces had to be adjusted to the change taking place in the rotation of the planet. The Greenwich Royal Observatory explained that small alterations had been noted in the rotation of the Earth, causing a difference between solar time and the official registered time. The new year would simply have one second added to it, but from then on adaptations would have to be made periodically.

This discrepancy between solar and registered time had been observed scientifically for twenty years, but only then was it being made public. The book, *The Fifth Race*,[20] revealed that a variation in the rotation of the planet was one of the conditions of planetary change: "With the shift in the inclination of the planet's magnetic axis, all life on the planet will change. Other changes may eventually be announced in the rotation of the planet, in its orbit, and in atmospheric pressure."

---

[20] See *The Fifth Race*, the works by Trigueirinho on page 123.

The book goes on to describe: "The days will be shorter. There will be periods instead of months; the names of those periods remain unrevealed, but they will be longer than the current months. What you call years will also be longer. Therefore, the method by which you now measure time will change radically. You will live much longer without your bodies undergoing the well-known deterioration which is currently natural to this level of existence."

The shift in the inclination of the magnetic axis can be accelerated by the way humans behave, which continuously alters the equilibrium of the planet. For example, when certain nuclear tests were being carried out, the media reported that North American and English scientists detonated a thermonuclear bomb in a desert area of the United States. This generated earth tremors felt in cities more than 100 miles away. The impact of the blast made the soil shoot up more than 300 feet. The explosion, equivalent to a moderate earthquake, registered 5.4 points on the Richter scale.

The crust of the Earth reacts to this violence, in one way or another. In fact, right after the thermonuclear bomb experiment, the Redoubt volcano, in Alaska, erupted for the *first* time in 25 years, shooting up clouds of ash and steam for more than 6 miles.

Deranged humans not only use the subsoil for nuclear tests, but also use people for experiments. Reports disclose that in some regions of Central Asia civilians have been used to study the effects of the radiation of atomic bombs.

The immediate consequences of such behavior seem obvious to us and indicate that today the forces of involution are confronting the constructive energies in their final battle. Even though it has been said since the time of the Book of Job:

Ask the birds of the sky,
and they will inform you;
or talk to the earth,
and it will teach you;
even the fish in the sea will tell you,

humans from the surface of the Earth continue to misuse free will.

Scientific research has shown that Australians are engaged in a contradictory undertaking of preserving the water that at the same time they are destroying. In order to maintain the system of life-supporting water on which they depend, they will have to deal with a chaotic and almost uncontrollable situation created by humanity itself.

Two hundred years ago a natural forest covered the territory watered by the great Murray River in southeast Australia. The deep roots of these trees absorbed great quantities of water from the subsoil. Since the time of European colonization, over 60% of those trees have been cut down to make way for farms, pastures and towns and have been replaced with shallow vegetation requiring less water.

The rainwater that in the past was absorbed by the trees began to cause the overflow of the natural subterranean systems of drainage, about 300 feet below the surface. The water levels rose and flooding began from the subsoil, bringing to surface salty residues from a very ancient seabed. Those salts are lethal to the remaining trees and to most plant and animal life. The subterranean areas of the Murray River basin store from one to six billion tons of salt that will increasingly destroy arable lands.

Another example of an irreversible imbalance is occurring in South America. When the flow of the Iguassú Falls, in southern Brazil, was rerouted, some regions suffered calamitous droughts and others, devastating floods. Although such facts are rarely associated with the forewarning of increasing catastrophes, the link between them is clear. We reaffirm these warnings because devastation will go on until the great cataclysm befalls.

♦ ♦ ♦

Atlantis, a continent which was submerged in one of the floods, appears for the first time in currently known literature in Plato's[21] writings. Events regarding the floods were recorded and guarded only by hermetic groups and modern exoteric world culture has very little data on them. However, the disappearance of ancient Atlantis became known publicly through the writings of Plato. Since then, the flood has been presented as a sort of punishment of the Atlanteans who had fallen into a state considered imperfect by the forces of evolution. It seems that after a long period of decadence, which culminated in involvement with various forms of magic, natural forces began to react, resulting in the cataclysm of the flood.

Plato's descriptions also reveal that the flood changed the location of the seas. The Mediterranean valley was flooded, while the waters that once covered all of North Africa shrank to the current Strait of Gibraltar. According to Plato, the region of the Mediterranean Sea used to be a fertile and humid valley, cut by four great rivers and the cradle of an advanced civilization. Vestiges may be seen in paintings found in certain parts of Southern Europe and Northern Africa.

---

[21] See Glossary.

According to Plato in his *Timaeus*, at that time one could traverse what is today a large sea. There was an island in front of the passage called the "Pillars of Hercules." That island was larger than Libya and Asia combined. And travelers of those times could cross from this island to others, and then reach the continent on the opposite coast of the sea, which truly deserved its name.

Plato was evidently referring to the lands of America when he wrote that one could reach "the entire continent on the opposite coast of that sea."

The narrative describes a powerful and "marvelous" empire in Atlantis, which ruled over the entire island, as well as many others and portions of the continent. But the earthquakes began, then the cataclysms and, according to Plato, "in the span of one single terrible day and night, everything was swallowed by the earth in one single blast, and the island of Atlantis sank into the sea and disappeared."

The fertility of that soil was better than any other, making it possible to feed multitudes with only a few inhabitants working on the land. The quality of the fruits and the vitality of the pastures could never be compared with those of today. The size of the harvest would be unbelievable even to the prosperous modern farmer.

In the Akashic records, Plato saw that Atlantis had very tall trees and lands full of inexhaustible pastures. According to his description, the water "did not flow wastefully, such as occurs today, to get lost in sterile lands and then roll into the sea. The earth received the water into its core, and from the sky it received an amount that it preserved within its layers made waterproof by clay." The water falling from higher places poured into cavities from where abundant and tranquil streamlets flowed all around, inspiring humans in their inner journeys.

According to Plato, that soil was tended by "true farmers." Working on the soil was not considered then, as it is today, a compulsory confinement. People were genuinely dedicated to farming. They loved beauty and enjoyed the serene and temperate seasons.

The sanctuaries on the physical level left by the peoples of those times were, for Plato's time, a testimony to the existence of this abundance and beauty.

The philosopher also mentioned that during a certain period there were kings in Atlantis who obeyed universal laws of evolution, "united with the divine principle" to which they were attuned, since those kings were not terrestrial but came from other spheres. They were broad-minded in all matters and when facing decisions, they used kindness, discernment and flexibility.

During their time on Earth, they utilized precious goods without becoming attached to them. The gold and riches which they used while on the physical level did not entice or allure them. They had great self-control and lived correctly. They highly valued the exercise of virtues and obedience to the Law. Plato said that these kings were clairvoyant and cultivated good relationships with almost everyone and considered material wealth of minor importance. With this conduct and with the "divine principle always evolving within them," they saw their material assets also increase without letting this influence them and without losing sight of their goal.

However, the time came when the divine principle "lessened

in those kings because of the repeated miscegenation with numerous mortal humans" from the Earth. Even though that principle had come from the cosmos, through prolonged contact with Earth, it ended up becoming mixed with material characteristics. In time, these traits took over the human character and from then on the kings were unable to handle material wealth without becoming influenced by it. Thus they succumbed to the condition of most terrestrial humans.

Other clairvoyants at the time denounced their perversions and consequently were persecuted and exterminated. Having eliminated the sages and people of vision, the Atlanteans began to lose precious opportunities for inner evolution. One of the "gods" of the time, who had the power to "know all things," saw the miserable path awaiting that once prosperous race. The people began forgetting a basic law: material goods come naturally to those who are disengaged and use them detachedly, but material goods control and enslave those who try to obtain them at all costs.

That race did not escape this immutable law. From the elevated race that they had been, they declined into a primitive state, incapable of self-restraint in anything whatsoever.

◆ ◆ ◆

The great floods came—several during the last nine thousand years. According to Plato, between one disaster and another, mudslides from the higher places flowed down without depositing much sediment and "rolling on, they ended up disappearing in the abyss." Compared to what it had been before, the Earth looked "like the skeleton of a body that had become scrawny from disease." The mild and prosperous regions of ancient times became like stripped carcasses. The prairies once carpeted in grasses and flowers, the mountains once cloaked in vast forests, lost their original appearance, they lost all their beauty.

The enormous trees vanished and the scrub covering the great mountains could feed only bees. Some humans then learned that "it is better to die in God than to reign over the Earth from one end to the other, for what is the use of possessing the whole world if one's soul is enslaved?"

When confronting the attractive force of everything that is densely material, "if you do not use your right hand as though it were your left, or what is above as though it were below, or that which went before as though it were to come, you will not know the real kingdom." This is what the sojourners in the vessel will always keep in mind. They will also know that "the measure you use will be applied to measure you. As you have judged, so will you be judged." These are immutable laws.

◆ ◆ ◆

Mythologies of different cultures and ages tell accounts of floods. Noah appears in several of these representing the new human of the race that comes after the disaster, the one who begins the work of populating the Earth again after the global purifications. Among the floods mentioned, there is that of Samothrace, prior to the time of the Argonauts, in which the whole country was submerged. In Greece, it is said that in the time of Deucalion, son of Prometheus, a flood occurred similar to the one narrated in the Bible. Deucalion and his wife, Pyrrha, were saved, for, like Noah, Deucalion built an ark and took shelter in it with his wife, children, and a pair of animals of each species.

Slavic mythology also tells of a flood, in which all of the

humanity of that era was drowned except for one man and one woman. "Don't you know that it takes only two healthy young people for the planet to be inhabited once more?" affirm the extraterrestrial beings of ERKS.[22]

Theosophy tells us that in Brazil there was a time when a certain "foreigner" caused everybody to die through great floods. Indian mythology, in turn, tells of a flood, and cites Vaivasvata Manu as the Noah. Likewise, in China there is the narrative of a flood that occurred during the days of Peirun, a man who was also saved with his family. The story of Xisuthrus, the Chaldean Noah, follows the same trend.

The consequences of conflictive human behavior are always the same. Nevertheless, it seems that in the opportunity which is approaching, the cycle of ignorance prevalent so far is about to be closed; a period of new awareness is opening. Philosophers and masters of wisdom have already disclosed studies and treatments of the so-called "illnesses of the soul."[23] But now a new factor has come in to help humans: the imbalances will be healed in Noah's immense laboratory space vessel.

According to Noah-Plato there are two main illnesses of the soul: one is madness and the other is ignorance. Excessive pleasures and pains are serious factors of imbalance. The middle path is to be found in sobriety, discernment and a spirit of service. There is no other option on planet Earth at this time. Experiencing pleasure or suffering to an extreme, such as most humans do today, after

---

[22] See *ERKS—Inner World*, the works by Trigueirinho on page 123.
[23] **Soul**, here, refers to the psychic part of humans, not to their deeper, non-material part.

having pursued such false precepts for several incarnations, in time leads one to madness.

Although some humans are considered perverse, in reality they are insane, explain Plato and the Noahs. As we can see, the viewpoint of the vessel does not always agree with medical, psychological and sociological concepts.

In the vessel it is a known fact that nobody is ignorant and corrupt because he or she wants to be that way or for the reasons that earthly science presupposes. If some people have such traits, this stems from the negative tendencies of certain earthly elements that entered into their constitution when they were being formed. According to Plato, in almost everyone's daily life, "man really does consider vice an enemy, but vice comes to him in spite of everything." Thus, the inner self may be greatly limited in its action in the three-dimensional world due to the individual's left side consciousness, the rational side. Human intellect has matured sufficiently to understand these things so it will find the strength to ward off what is detrimental.

◆ ◆ ◆

"But God the builder placed our head at the top and gave the whole body its vertical posture," says Noah through Plato. However, ever since the beginning humans remained outside of the laws; they used only the lower part of their body, to the point of devitalizing it. According to Plato, a person who has cultivated love of science and truthful thoughts and of all the faculties has mainly exercised the ability to think about immortal and divine things, such a person can participate consciously in the state of immortality and fully reap its benefits.

Plato speaks like Noah: when someone worships the divine incessantly, the god that dwells within him enjoys well-being, thus it is inevitable that he should be especially happy.

Four hundred and twenty one years before Christ, Plato had already referred to the development of the right side consciousness. He taught that the movements which have an affinity with the divine principle in us are the thoughts of the All and its circumvolutions. We are to follow the movements related to what is to come, which are in our heads and which were disturbed, and must be re-established through knowledge of harmony and of the movements of the All. Those who contemplate should become similar to the object of their contemplation, according to its original nature. In doing so, they should attain, for both the present and the future, that complete perfection of life which the gods proposed to humans.

It is evident that, in general, this civilization has not yet attained this intent, for only a minority has stood out from the amorphous mass of humanity. This is why Noah's vessel—where the "gods" work—has arrived. In the vessel each human, as a potential god, will finally find his or her true fellow beings and will never feel alone.

THIRD PART

Questions from Students

Will the humans who are going to transmigrate to other planets after the transmigration carry with them the permanent atoms[24] of each of their bodies?

The human physical, emotional and mental bodies that have been previously prepared will have such subtle atoms that they will be able to adapt to the new state awaiting them, either on other planets or in immense space vessels. Once they have regained their awareness in the new habitat, the transmigrants will recognize their bodies and they will also perceive clearly the changes that have taken place.

Only those who have known how to prepare themselves during the lengthy period of purification, by the methods given to them, will be transferred or transmigrated. The permanent atoms of the bodies that have been duly prepared will be transferred or transmigrated.

With the development of the right side consciousness, a state

---

[24] See Glossary.

which is also intuitive, it is possible to participate in the formation of the new sheaths (or bodies), based upon what was achieved qualitatively during the stages of purification. Those new bodies will be used unless the current ones have become subtle enough to be adapted.

◆ ◆ ◆

Since the humans of the new race will have a different physical birthing process, how will their emotional and mental bodies be formed? Will they exist, like the physical body?

The emotional body appertaining to this three-dimensional world will almost disappear for it will merge with the mental body and together they will become a harmonious unit. This amalgamation will be governed by the laws of higher consciousness and not by the laws of the Earth and its environs, such as still happens today.

When the emotional body enters into a harmonious unification with the already purified mental body, its struggle to prevail over the individual will disappear. The mental body, having awakened to its true Light and now unified with the emotional body, will develop without the attachments and crystallizations imposed on it by the laws that govern the left side consciousness, the rational state.

The emotional body will follow the development of the individual's higher mental body. There will no longer be conflict between one body and another, but rather the natural functioning of the higher mind unified with a now elevated emotional body that will be free, including of the disorders of the physical body itself. At this point of the process of evolution the physical body, no longer a source of imbalance, will also have been purified and will have received a new genetic code, making it a genuine vehicle and instrument for the more subtle bodies.

◆ ◆ ◆

What will the relationship between human beings and Nature be like?

In more advanced civilizations such as some intraterrestrial ones, Nature is controlled by humans who know the laws of supra-nature. They have reached this stage because in previous cycles they were attuned with the natural laws. On intraterrestrial levels there is perfect harmony between humans and the environment. For instance, nobody would ever think of artificially redirecting the course of a river or some body of water. They know that the paths followed by water, whether on the surface or inside the Earth, have a balancing, mineralizing and purifying function. To change them would mean to break down the equilibrium created by the wise and encompassing laws of supra-nature—which is the very Nature we know today only at a more advanced stage of evolution.

Just as there is a supraphysical level, there is the supraphysical nature, governed by laws which humans of the surface of the Earth still have not recognized. These laws cannot be revealed to the majority as yet, because they would be used to escalate the present imbalance. As humans develop their right side consciousness, they will receive direct and intuitive knowledge and they will thus be able to perceive different aspects of their surrounding worlds.

The evolution of humans will be accompanied by the manifestation of new species of the plant kingdom, with fruit trees that will bear plentifully without being limited to times and seasons, as they are now. Within the law of harmony, each region will supply the energy needed for the people there. This will be possible because human actions will have ceased to disrupt the natural balance in which plants produce what they are meant to produce within the laws of abundance and in attunement with an evolutionary plan.

The cycles of the plants are currently out of control due to instability of the weather since the laws for the climate have been altered through human interference. But after the global purification of the surface of the Earth, cereals and fruits will be produced homogeneously throughout the regions of the planet. Interchange of these goods will also be possible, but never based upon the craving for what is superfluous.

Today all kinds of seeds are sown in any area, without taking into account the characteristics that would be more appropriate for their development. In an orderly life, people will know the best areas for each type of seed and so the different regions of the planet will produce specific crops. Fraternal barter, aimed at mutual aid and shunning exploitation, will be essential. The concept of the "producer," so prevalent in this civilization, will vanish from daily life since interest in profit and surplus will be extinguished. People will become aware of the cooperation that should prevail among kingdoms and of their personal responsibility as mental-spiritual beings.

Pleasant cities and towns will replace the countless countries that currently clash over territorial claims; with their fears and conflicts, they provoke traumatic magnetic imbalances in the planet and in Nature. Violent rainstorms or hurricanes will cease to exist when humans are no longer greedy and self-centered. Humans will stop destroying Nature therefore it will no longer use violence to regain its balance and to serve as warnings that, nevertheless, are still disregarded. The rains will not be destructive as they are today, the outcome of an energy imbalance, but will come to nurture the soil and to give life to the creatures of all the kingdoms

Seaquakes and earthquakes will disappear from the face of the Earth for a few millennia. As people stop eating fish, they will no longer bring on today's devastating action of the seas and the rivers when waters shift and overflow in order to convey messages, the symbolism of which is not understood.

Water will not only quench thirst, it will also purify the organism. It will recover its ancient healing function and will contain vitaminic properties which are presently inconceivable.

New types of plants are already being created in the laboratory space vessels some of which are being tested on the Earth as they are gradually introduced into the botany of certain regions free from disharmony. These experiments are being conducted by highly evolved beings in order to provide future humans with healing, sustenance and harmonization, whenever needed, as well as to maintain the purity of the atmosphere.

Evolved beings are preparing to incarnate on Earth, bringing a clear idea of what their tasks are to be, principally with the plant kingdom. This will bring about significant changes, including in people's form of nutrition.

◆ ◆ ◆

Is the technological level achieved by a race consonant with its level of evolution?

No. Humanity can develop a powerful technology without a corresponding development of consciousness. Thus it uses its discoveries destructively, such as is happening once again on this planet. Among many examples, it is widely known that in 1987 the Chernobyl nuclear reactor was damaged in the worst recorded nuclear accident. The number of victims was incalculable and hundreds of thousands of residents had to be evacuated from the area. Radioactive leakage persists despite the thousand-ton protective concrete vault and its deleterious consequences have never been made public.

Notorious cases such as Chernobyl, and the hazardous conditions of many other nuclear plants, remain suppressed, showing that technological development without a development of consciousness will immerse the planet in uncontrollable contamination. According to revealed documentation, this is the last time humanity of the surface of the Earth will carry out experiments in advanced technology without evolving in character and consciousness.

◆ ◆ ◆

Could it be that teachers incarnated in India who still use systems of meditation that focus on the chakras[25] are misled?

This is another typical case of individuals using techniques without first working on their character and consciousness.

---

[25] See Glossary.

In the past, meditation on the chakras was only given to students under the supervision of a competent teacher. In modern times that basic precept gradually gave way to the commercialization of yoga and of so-called spiritual education. The occult processes then began to circulate publicly, causing imbalances in many people.

No knowledgeable teacher today would focus meditation on the chakras, not even under the former requirements. In humans, the energy system of the chakras corresponds to the stage of development of the left side consciousness. For the planet, it corresponds to the cycle of the masculine polarity represented not only by the human chakras, but also by the Orient, such as India and its teachers from the past.

Now that the feminine polarity of the planet is entering into special activity in order to balance the energy of the masculine polarity developed in the past cycle, the chakra system is deactivating and the human energy circuit is beginning to follow the new planetary cycle.

In humans, the energy circuit that corresponds to the planetary feminine polarity is the development of the right side consciousness centers: the right side mental center, the right side heart center and the right side cosmic plexus, which is situated at the level of the last rib on the right. The awakening of this circuit is linked to the overall shift in the planet's polarity.

The true teachers who helped people develop the chakras have already disincarnated, since they have finished their task. Having completed their cycle of teaching on Earth, they have gone on to other levels, transmigrated to other planets, or have been assigned to a new task at their present level of consciousness.

If by chance some teachers still adhere to the previous aims, either they have ceased to receive light in their work or they are still helping some people who cannot keep up with energy shifts of the planet and therefore still need techniques that have been superseded by those who are developing the right side consciousness.

Most probably there are no teachers of really advanced evolution in such cases. The most evolved finish their tasks in accordance with the principal planetary movements. They never go counter to the plans inspired by the Sublime Intelligences of the Intergalactic Confederation and the Central Celestial Government, which true teachers know *inwardly*.

However, there are still some teachers of average evolution who are active on the planet without any such links with elevated spiritual energies. It is not up to us to judge them. If this is still permitted it is because a Greater Intelligence has determined that some earthly humans be tested. It is only when faced with a test that one can manifest one's true predisposition, one's real position in regard to LIFE and the SUBSTANCE that sheathes it.

"And gathering his disciples upon the Mount of Olives, Jesus spoke to them of the Antichrist. And of how the unjust would be separated from the just, as the shepherd separates the sheep from the ram."

At the end He said: "Do not be disturbed."

Glossary

APOCRYPHAL

Today this term has taken on the connotation of something false, falsified and not scholarly. However, in its original sense, it meant *occult*, namely, restricted to a few. The apocryphal texts were read by a minority. Today the "Apocryphal Gospels" and the "Apocryphal Bible" are widely known; the new manuscripts discovered and disseminated are no longer under the control of organized religions or sects. Almost all the citations given in this book in reference to the Gospels were taken from apocryphal texts, attributed to the disciples of Jesus or to anonymous authors.

It is known that the Vatican libraries have miles of bookshelves full of works that have never been revealed to the wider public. Among them are important documents the contents of which have never reached the conscious knowledge of humans of the surface of the Earth.

◆ ◆ ◆

ASTRAL DEATH

In this book the term *astral death* describes the state experienced by those who, once having left the physical body, then leave their astral-emotional body. This is equivalent to a second "death." The evacuees who are taken into Noah's vessel will not go through this experience. Some of them will return to the surface of the Earth using the same bodies which have been harmonized, while the more evolved will transcend the astral level.

◆ ◆ ◆

ATLANTIS

This continent, which submerged, once occupied the area corresponding to the present Atlantic Ocean. According to Theosophy, it was inhabited by the race that preceded the current one, in which the emotional body of humans was developed. After that civilization reached its zenith, people there began developing psychic forces and controlling them for selfish reasons. This practice of black magic produced the cataclysm. Esoteric culture explains cataclysms as the reaction of Nature and the evolutionary energies, which always end up freeing humans from the obstacles that impede their higher development. Helena Blavatsky affirmed that the cataclysm that destroyed Atlantis happened thousands of years ago. Although the date may not be precise, Blavatsky, who was an initiate, can be considered one of the most reliable sources of information not limited to the scientific-rational circles.

Reincarnated beings from ancient Atlantis can be found nowadays in the government of a great modern power that is also using black magic to maintain the country's economic stability. Just as in the past, these tactics are not succeeding. According to the forecasts of the plans for planetary transmigration, that country will be one of the first to be submerged during the coming holocaust that will be aggravated by the way humans behave.

◆ ◆ ◆

BLAVATSKY

Helena Petrovna Blavatsky (1831-1891) was a mystic whose tasks included providing humans with a basis for occult wisdom, thus permitting them to develop a synthesis of various spiritual tendencies of the planet. She articulated the teachings inspired by the planetary Hierarchy, addressing preparation for the next phases of the Earth. Her well known monumental work, *The Secret Doctrine*, was written with the cooperation of ascended masters, beings of a high evolution who belong to the Fraternity of Evolutionary Energies, also known today as the Intergalactic Confederation which is affiliated with the Central Celestial Government.

Among other things, her books served to unmask a number of traditional fallacies (some engendered by human ignorance itself, others premeditatedly introduced by different theologies), and to break the materialism embodied by this civilization. Her work and her presence on the physical level contributed to the release of millions of beings from the closed circle maintained by cultural, philosophic and religious obscurantism. It is known that *The Secret Doctrine* greatly influenced thinkers, and in a special way, the physicist Albert Einstein.

◆ ◆ ◆

CHAKRAS

These energy centers function in the etheric body of humans who are still under the law of material karma. When people transcend this law, they become governed by the higher aspects of the Law of Evolution and are no longer conditioned by the forces of these centers.

Chakras respond to the energies that govern planetary life. Humans are linked to those energies through the chakras and thus are enabled to participate in some way in broader rhythms. However, the individuals who have renounced free will make this link through the energy centers of the right side consciousness and no longer, as most of humanity, through the chakras taught by ancient doctrines.

◆ ◆ ◆

ERKS

ERKS, a Planetary Center that is projected in a supraphysical intraterrestrial region of Córdoba, in Argentina, is integrated with two other Centers: Miz Tli Tlan (a supraphysical intraterrestrial area of the Peruvian Andes) and Aurora (an intraterrestrial area in Salto, Uruguay). These supraphysical nuclei constitute a subtle network of communication and transmission of pure energies which permeate all manifested life.

ERKS consists of an intraterrestrial civilization and of extraterrestrial beings who have come as remainders from other galaxies to contribute to the great change the race of the surface of the Earth will undergo. When necessary, these beings take on physical bodies. ERKS is also one of the largest bases of operations designated to carry out the transmigration of rescuable beings on planet Earth, which is about to face a global cataclysm. On the inner levels of consciousness ERKS also works with the initiation of humans into supraphysical knowledge.

Books by Trigueirinho dealing with this intraterrestrial center include: *ERKS—Inner World; Signs of Contact; New Signs of Contact* and *The Space Gardeners*.

◆ ◆ ◆

PERMANENT ATOM

Before each incarnation, a particle called the permanent atom attracts others of the same quality to form the earthly bodies of humans. Permanent atoms are in contact with the individual's causal body, which up to a certain stage, holds the memory of past lives and therefore knows what type of matter will be needed in successive lives. It is clear that these atoms are present in those who are still under the law of reincarnation.

◆ ◆ ◆

PLATO

An initiate who lived in Greece 400 years before the Christian era, Plato was dedicated to philosophy, the arts, geometry, mathematical calculations, and to teaching. He was one of the greatest philosophers to ever have incarnated on Earth, and one of the most distinguished among the Greeks. He was later depreciated by the rationalists, mainly because he presented reincarnation as a reality. His explanations about the inner world of humans provided a solid foundation for the formation of countless spiritualists all over the world. In the philosophy he formulated, God is the cause and the substance as the Logos or the Word which contains the eternal ideas. Plato pondered on the archetypes and showed that humans have a divine origin. Immortality and the possibility for humans to attain a more subtle consciousness were ever-recurring themes in his innumerable writings, which today have been translated into almost all the languages that have an elevated level of thought.

Among his works are: *Timaeus, Crito, Phaedo, Phaedrus, The Banquet,*

Gorgias, Euthyphro, Pythagoras, Laws, and *The Republic*. In *Timaeus* and in *Crito* he provided information about Atlantis, a continent where the previous race developed emotional characteristics, typical of a civilization confined to the terrestrial astral level.

The Ancient Academy, or the Platonic school of thought, was also based on the principles of purity of life and nobility of character inspired by Plato. Plato based himself upon these principles, which were considered indispensable for all, without distinction. Today's "academies" have lost these moral principles. His school was widely criticized, mainly by the theology created later to satisfy the masses of the Christian era. This theology, while presenting spiritual law to people, also allowed for subterfuges, so that the priestly cast and the ecclesiastical hierarchy could justify their lifestyle.

◆ ◆ ◆

RUDOLF STEINER

Austrian philosopher Rudolf Steiner, (1861-1925), a highly evolved being, brought philosophical-spiritual insights to many sectors of human life, such as medicine, pharmacology, agriculture, and others. Within the sphere of his "spiritual science," he developed the concept of the "self" as a channel for energies from spiritual dimensions. His entire approach accentuates the existence of an individuality with a divine nature that is present within each human. The extensive writings based on his lectures are disseminated in various countries.

◆ ◆ ◆

THAYKHUMA

Major Regent of the Mirrors, a system of communication that represents an elevated state of intergalactic consciousness, Thaykhuma is also the fifth Hierarchy in Miz Tli Tlan, the supraphysical intraterrestrial center located in the Peruvian Andes, which is currently the center of the inner government of planet Earth.

Mirrors are focal points of energy activated by a higher source. Currently the work with Mirrors is carried out by feminine beings who pick up the movement of the forces and keep them under control so that the laws may be fulfilled. The energy wave that activates the Mirrors branches out into a vast field that corresponds to the evolutionary state of each being and adapts to it while helping it to make adaptations. Although the energy field is generalized, it also attends to each individual because each one receives according to his or her Hierarchy, task, evolution and designated role in the plan of evolution.

Intraterrestrial civilizations are in charge of the work with the Mirrors and in due time this work will also be taken on by humans from the surface of the Earth. Groups linked to this work that may already exist on the surface of the planet are hermetic and designated by the Hierarchy which cautions that they should remain completely concealed.

More information on the work of the Mirrors may be found in the books *Miz Tli Tlan—an Awakening World*; *New Signs of Contact* and *Calling Humanity*, by Trigueirinho.

References

"And the one who has been inspirited from within will come forward and explain the words of true wisdom."

Apocryphal Gospel of Valentine

The New Oxford Annotated Bible with Apocrypha [Oxford University Press USA, 1977, Herbert May and Bruce Metzer, Eds,]

The Collected Dialogues of Plato [Princeton, N.J.: Princeton University Press, Bollingen Series, 1961, Edith Hamilton, Huntingdon Cairne, Lane Cooper, Eds.]

Mother's Agenda, [Chambly, QC: Institut de Recherches Evolutives Canada, 1981]

Rudolf Steiner, *The Gospel of Mark* – from a series of lectures 1912 [Steinerbooks, Kalmia Bittleston, Trans.]

Roudolf Steiner, *The Gospel of John* – from a series of lectures 1908 [Floris Book, Kalmia Bittleston, Trans.]

Roudolf Steiner, *The Gospel of Matthew* – from a series of lectures 1910 [Floris Books, Kalmia Bittleston, Trans.]

Rudolf Steiner, *According to Luke* (previously published as *The Gospel of Luke*)—*lectures in Dornach, September 1900, The Gospel of Compassion and Love Revealed* [SteinerBooks, Catherine E. Creeger, Trans., Robert McDermott, Intro.].

Paul Brunton, *Perspectives—The Timeless Way of Wisdom* [Burdett, New York: Larson Publications, 1984]

About Trigueirinho and His Work

Jose Trigueirinho Netto (1931-2018) was born in Sao Paulo, Brazil. He lived in Europe for a number of years, where he maintained contact with individuals who were advanced on the spiritual path, including Paul Brunton.

In his own life he was an example of the teachings that he transmitted through his books and talks about the transcendence and elevation of the human being, the contact with the soul and with even more profound nuclei of the being, impersonal service, and the link with the Spiritual Hierarchies.

One of the fundamental elements of his work is to stimulate the expansion of human consciousness and to liberate it from the bonds that keep it imprisoned to material aspects of existence, both external and internal.

He was the Founder of the Community of Light Figueira (http://www.comunidadefigueira.org.br) and a Founder and member of the Board of Directors of the Fraternity International

Humanitarian Federation (www.fraterinternacional) as well as a Co-Founder of the Grace Mercy Order, an ecumenical Christian monastic order. He also was an active collaborator, instructor and spiritual protector of three other communities located in Uruguay, Argentina and Portugal.

In his last 30 years he lived in the Community of Light Figueira, in the interior of Minas Gerais, Brazil, a community that at present has approximately 300 residents and which is visited annually by thousands of collaborators who are members of a larger network of humanitarian services and of spiritual studies that was always guided and followed closely by Trigueirinho.

Thanks to his inestimable instruction and his love for the Kingdoms of Nature and as a result of the exemplary work that he himself implanted in the Figueira community, the Animal, Vegetable and Mineral Kingdoms are the recipients of loving treatment there.

Trigueirinho wrote over 80 books, published originally in Portuguese, with many of them translated into Spanish, English, French and German. He gave more than 3,000 talks that were recorded live and which are available in CD, with some available in DVD and pen drive. Approximately 100 of these recorded talks are available with English voice over at the website of the Shasti Association: http://www.shasti.org/instruction (drop down the menu tab titled "Trigueirinho Instruction" and then click on "MP3 audios").

The primary focus of the first phase of Trigueirinho's work was concerned with self-knowledge, prayer, instruction and spiritual transformation. Following this, he began to transmit information with respect to Universal Life and about the assistance that humanity has from its beginnings received by means of the Intra-terrestrial White Brotherhood which inhabits the Retreats and the Planetary Centers as well as through the Cosmic Brotherhood of the Universe. He provides information about the presence of the Spiritual Hierarchy on the planet and the advent of the new humanity.

His work also includes themes relating to: the need for humanity to balance the negative karmas that it has created in relation to the Kingdoms of Nature; the negative karmic burden that we carry from the history of slavery and the genocide of indigenous peoples; and the nature of spiritual work in groups. He also addresses issues of healing, a larger vision of astrology, the esoteric nature of symbols, sound and colors, and the divine feminine.

In his last eight years he analyzed with clarity and with the wisdom that always characterized him, the messages that the Divinity has been giving to the planet as a warning to humanity (available from www.mensajerosdivinos.org/en).

His work reveals a real comprehension of the significance of all the Kingdoms of Nature on our planet, the true spiritual task of the human being, its place in the universe and also its responsibility before Creation.

Finally, he clarifies the reasons for the crisis that today is devastating humanity, teaching how to avoid reacting negatively to an immanent natural catastrophe by contacting more subtle levels of consciousness, and opening perspectives for the beginning of a more luminous cycle for our race.

About Trigueirinho and His Work

Jose Trigueirinho Netto (1931-2018) was born in Sao Paulo, Brazil. He lived in Europe for a number of years, where he maintained contact with individuals who were advanced on the spiritual path, including Paul Brunton.

In his own life he was an example of the teachings that he transmitted through his books and talks about the transcendence and elevation of the human being, the contact with the soul and with even more profound nuclei of the being, impersonal service, and the link with the Spiritual Hierarchies.

One of the fundamental elements of his work is to stimulate the expansion of human consciousness and to liberate it from the bonds that keep it imprisoned to material aspects of existence, both external and internal.

He was the Founder of the Community of Light Figueira (http://www.comunidadefigueira.org.br) and a Founder and member of the Board of Directors of the Fraternity International

Humanitarian Federation (www.fraterinternacional) as well as a Co-Founder of the Grace Mercy Order, an ecumenical Christian monastic order. He also was an active collaborator, instructor and spiritual protector of three other communities located in Uruguay, Argentina and Portugal.

In his last 30 years he lived in the Community of Light Figueira, in the interior of Minas Gerais, Brazil, a community that at present has approximately 300 residents and which is visited annually by thousands of collaborators who are members of a larger network of humanitarian services and of spiritual studies that was always guided and followed closely by Trigueirinho.

Thanks to his inestimable instruction and his love for the Kingdoms of Nature and as a result of the exemplary work that he himself implanted in the Figueira community, the Animal, Vegetable and Mineral Kingdoms are the recipients of loving treatment there.

Trigueirinho wrote over 80 books, published originally in Portuguese, with many of them translated into Spanish, English, French and German. He gave more than 3,000 talks that were recorded live and which are available in CD, with some available in DVD and pen drive. Approximately 100 of these recorded talks are available with English voice over at the website of the Shasti Association: http://www.shasti.org/instruction (drop down the menu tab titled "Trigueirinho Instruction" and then click on "MP3 audios").

The primary focus of the first phase of Trigueirinho's work was concerned with self-knowledge, prayer, instruction and spiritual transformation. Following this, he began to transmit information with respect to Universal Life and about the assistance that humanity has from its beginnings received by means of the Intra-terrestrial White Brotherhood which inhabits the Retreats and the Planetary Centers as well as through the Cosmic Brotherhood of the Universe. He provides information about the presence of the Spiritual Hierarchy on the planet and the advent of the new humanity.

His work also includes themes relating to: the need for humanity to balance the negative karmas that it has created in relation to the Kingdoms of Nature; the negative karmic burden that we carry from the history of slavery and the genocide of indigenous peoples; and the nature of spiritual work in groups. He also addresses issues of healing, a larger vision of astrology, the esoteric nature of symbols, sound and colors, and the divine feminine.

In his last eight years he analyzed with clarity and with the wisdom that always characterized him, the messages that the Divinity has been giving to the planet as a warning to humanity (available from www.mensajerosdivinos.org/en).

His work reveals a real comprehension of the significance of all the Kingdoms of Nature on our planet, the true spiritual task of the human being, its place in the universe and also its responsibility before Creation.

Finally, he clarifies the reasons for the crisis that today is devastating humanity, teaching how to avoid reacting negatively to an immanent natural catastrophe by contacting more subtle levels of consciousness, and opening perspectives for the beginning of a more luminous cycle for our race.

Books by Trigueirinho

(Books available in English have English title first)

Published by Editora Pensamento
Sao Paulo, Brazil

1987

NOSSA VIDA NOS SONHOS
OUR LIFE IN DREAMS

A ENERGIA DOS RAIOS EM NOSSA VIDA
THE ENERGY OF THE RAYS IN OUR LIVES

1988

DO IRREAL AO REAL
FROM THE UNREAL TO THE REAL

HORA DE CRESCER INTERIORMENTE
O Mito de Hércules Hoje
TIME FOR INNER GROWTH – *The Myth of Hercules Today*

A MORTE SEM MEDO E SEM CULPA
DEATH WITHOUT FEAR AND WITHOUT GUILT

CAMINHOS PARA A CURA INTERIOR
PATHS TO INNER HEALING

1989

ERKS – *Mundo Interno*
ERKS – *The Inner World*

Miz Tli Tlan – *Um Mundo que Desperta*
MIZ TLI TLAN – *A World that Awakens*

Aurora – Essência Cósmica Curadora
AURORA – *Cosmic Essence of Healing*

Signs of Contact
SINAIS DE CONTATO

O Novo Começo do Mundo
THE NEW BEGINNING OF THE WORLD

A Quinta Raça
THE FIFTH RACE

Padrões de conduta para a nova Humanidade
PATTERNS OF CONDUCT FOR THE NEW HUMANITY

Novos Sinais de Contato
NEW SIGNS OF CONTACT

Os Jardineiros do Espaço
THE SPACE GARDENERS

1990

A Busca da Síntese
THE SEARCH FOR SYNTHESIS

Noah's Vessel
A NAVE DE NOÉ

TEMPO DE RETIRO E TEMPO DE VIGÍLIA
A TIME OF RETREAT AND A TIME OF VIGIL

1991

PORTAS DO COSMOS
GATEWAYS OF THE COSMOS

ENCONTRO INTERNO – *A Consciência-Nave*
INNER ENCOUNTER – *The Consciousness Space Vessel*

A HORA DO RESGATE
THE TIME OF RESCUE

O LIVRO DOS SINAIS
THE BOOK OF SIGNS

MIRNA JAD – *Santuário Interior*
MIRNA JAD – *Inner Sanctuary*

AS CHAVES DE OURO
THE GOLDEN KEYS

1992

DAS LUTAS À PAZ
FROM STRUGGLE TO PEACE

A MORADA DOS ELISÍOS THE ELYSIAN DWELLING PLACE

HORA DE CURAR – *A Existência Oculta*
TIME FOR HEALING – *The Occult Existence*

O RESSURGIMENTO DE FÁTIMA LIS
THE RESURGENCE OF FATIMA LIS

História Escrita nos Espelhos
Princípios de Comunicação Cósmic
HISTORY WRITTEN IN THE MIRRORS -
Principles of Cosmic Communication

Passos Atuais
STEPS FOR NOW

Viagem por Mundos Sutis
TRAVEL THROUGH SUBTLE WORLDS

Segredos Desvelados – *Iberah e Anu Tea*
UNVEILED SECRETS – *Iberah and Anu Tea*

A Criação – *Nos Caminhos da Energia*
CREATION – *On the Paths of Energy*

The Mystery of the Cross In the Present Planetary Transition
O MISTÉRIO DA CRUZ NA ATUAL TRANSIÇÃO PLANETÁRIA

O Nascimento da Humanidade Futura
THE BIRTH OF THE FUTURE HUMANITY

1993

Aos Que Despertam
TO THOSE WHO AWAKEN

Paz Interna em Tempos Críticos
INNER PEACE IN CRITICAL TIMES

A Formação de Curadores
THE FORMATION OF HEALERS

Profecias aos Que Não Temem Dizer Sim
PROPHECIES FOR THOSE WHO ARE NOT AFRAID TO SAY YES

The Voice of Amhaj
A VOZ DE AMHAJ

O Visitante – O Caminho Para Anu Tea
THE VISITOR – *The Way to Anu Tea*

A Cura da Humanidade
THE HEALING OF HUMANITY

Os Números e a Vidas – *Uma Nova Compreensão da Simbologia Oculta nos Números*
NUMBERS AND LIFE – *A New Understanding of Occult Symbolism in Numbers*

Niskalkat – *Uma Mensagem para os Tempos de Emergência*
NISKALKAT – *A Message for Times of Emergency*

Encontros Com a Paz
ENCOUNTERS WITH PEACE

Novos Oráculos
NEW ORACLES

Um Novo Impulso Astrológico
A NEW ASTROLOGICAL IMPULSE

1994

Bases do Mundo Ardente – *Indicações para Contato com os Mundos suprafíscicos*
BASES OF THE FIERY WORLD – *Indications for Contacts with Supraphysical Worlds*

Contatos com um Monastério Interaterreno
CONTACTS WITH AN INTRATERRESTRIAL MONASTERY

Os oceanos têm Ouvidos
OCEANS HAVE EARS

A Trajetória do Fogo
THE PATH OF FIRE

Glossário Esotérico
ESOTERIC LEXICON

1995

The Light Within You
A LUZ DENTRO DE TI

1996

Doorway to a Kingdom
PORTAL PARA UM REINO

Beyond Karma
ALÉM DO CARMA

1997

We Are Not Alone
NÃO ESTAMOS SÓS

Winds of the spirit
VENTOS DO ESPÍRITO

Finding the Temple
O ENCONTRO DO TEMPLO

There is Peace
A PAZ EXISTE

1998

Path Without Shadows

CAMINHO SEM SOMBRAS

Mensagens para Uma Vida de Harmonia

MESSAGES FOR A LIFE OF HARMONY

1999

Toque Divino

THE DIVINE TOUCH

Coleçào Pedaços de Céu

  BITS FROM HEAVEN COLLECTION

- **Aromas do Espaço**
  AROMAS FROM SPACE
- **Nova Vida Bate à Porta**
  A NEW LIFE AWAITS YOU
- **Mais Luz No Horizonte**
  MORE LIGHT ON THE HORIZON
- **O Campanário Cósmico**
  THE COSMIC CAMPANILE
- **Nada Nos Falta**
  WE LACK NOTHING
- **Sagrados Mistérios**
  SACRED MYSTERIES
- **Ilhas de Salvaçáo**
  ISLANDS OF SALVATION

2002

Calling Humanity

  UM CHAMADO ESPECIAL

2004

ÉS VIAJANTE CÓSMICO
YOU ARE A COSMIC WAYFARER

IMPULSOS
IMPULSES

2005

PENSAMENTOS PARA TODO O ANO
THOUGHTS FOR THE WHOLE YEAR

2006

TRABALHO ESPIRITUAL COM A MENTE
SPIRITUAL WORK WITH THE MIND

**Published by Editora Irdin
Carmo da Cachoeira, Minas Gerais, Brazil**

2009

SIGNS OF BLAVATSKY – *An Unusual Encounter for the Present Time*
SINAIS DE BLAVATSKY – *Um Inusitado Encontro nos Dias de Hoje*

2012

CONSCIÊNCIAS E HIERARQUIAS
CONSCIOUSNESSES AND HIERARCHIES

2015

Mensagens Reunidas
COLLECTED MESSAGES

Mensagens para Sua Tranformaçã
MESSAGES FOR YOUR TRANSFORMATION

2017

Páginas de Amor e Compreensão
PAGES OF LOVE AND COMPREHENSION

2018

Novos Tempos: Nova Postura
NEW TIMES: NEW ATTITUDE

2020

Versos Livres
OBRA PÓSTUMA

Trigueirinho's works are published by:

Associação Irdin Editora – www.irdin.org.br (selected titles of books in English, Spanish and Portuguese and CDs in several languages), Carmo da Cachoeira, MG, Brazil.

Editora Pensamento – www.pensamento-cultrix.com.br (titles in Portuguese), São Paulo, SP, Brazil

Editorial Kier – www.kier.com.ar (selected titles in Spanish), Buenos Aires, Argentina.

Lichtwelle-Verlag – www.lichtwelle-verlag.ch (selected titles in Spanish and German), Zurich, Switzerland.

Shasti Association – www.shasti.org (selected titles in English), Mount Shasta, CA, USA

Lectures of Trigueirinho with Simultaneous English Translation

During over thirty years as Founder of the Figueira Community of Light, Trigueirinho gave bi-weekly lectures (called 'parthilha's or 'sharings') that were recorded live. Audience members were invited to submit questions to him which were placed in a small box and brought to him by an attendant. Arriving early, Trigueirinho sat at the lectern, reading through and taking notes on the audience questions. Thus, his lectures often began with the phrase "someone has asked a question...." After addressing some of these questions, he continued with the theme chosen for the day.

Approximately 70 of these 'sharings' were later dubbed with English translations. His voice or the translators can be augmented or diminished by adjusting the right-left balance of the recording.

To access these audio recordings go to: www.shasti.org/instruction, then drop down the menu tab titled "Trigueirinho Instruction" and then click on "MP3 audios."

A Book to Be Written
A New Viewpoint of the Monad
Alopathic and Homeopathic Medicine
An Esoteric Dimension of Power
An Overview of Current Life
Angels and Humanity – 1
Angels and Humanity – 2
Angels and Humanity – 3
Angels and Humanity – 4
Bases of the Fiery World
Beyond Fire by Friction
Beyond Imperfection
Causal Body
Colors in Healing and the Formation of Our Light Vessel
Deep Healing
From the Human Kingdom to the Spiritual Kingdom
Getting through Today's Critical Times
Harmonization and Androgyny
How One Begins to Perceive One's Inner Self
How to Understand the Planetary Disasters
Human Trials | The Trials of the Soul
Information on the New Earth and the New Humanity
Inner and Outer Figueira
Instruction: a Step beyond Teaching
Liberating and Healing through Colors
Life in Cosmic Signs
New Supraterrestrial Pathways – 1
New Supraterrestrial Pathways – 2
New Supraterrestrial Pathways – 3
New Supraterrestrial Pathways – 4
Niskalkat
Noah's Vessel
On Vitality
Our Response to the Cosmos – 1
Our Response to the Cosmos – 2
Our Response to the Cosmos – 3
Our Response to the Cosmos – 4
Our Response to the Cosmos – 5
Our Response to the Cosmos – 6
Preparation for the Path of Initiation
Reflections on Illusion and Rescue
Reflections on Inner Attunement
Seeds of Inner Transformation
Seeking to Understand the Self

Several Levels of Spiritual Reading
Special Paths and the Path of the Majority
Spiritual Entities and Hierarchies
Spiritual Trials
Strengthening the Bases for the New Cycles
Subtle Bodies and Templing
Supraterrestrial Pathways – 1
Supraterrestrial Pathways – 2
Supraterrestrial Pathways – 3
Supraterrestrial Pathways – 4
Syntheses, Struggles and New Instructions
Taking Charge of One's Process of Dying – 1
Taking Charge of One's Process of Dying – 2
Taking Charge of One's Process of Dying – 3
The Art of Living in Current Times
The Cosmic Signs Reveal the Teaching – 1
The Cosmic Signs Reveal the Teaching – 2
The Desert
The Earth – Degeneration and Deliverance
The Era of the Gigantic Wave
The Importance of Self-Control in Epidemics
  and Other Risk Situations
The Light That Permeates Matter
The Mystery of the Cross in the Present
  Planetary Transition
The Doorways of the Planet – 1
The Doorways of the Planet – 2
The Doorways of the Planet – 3
The Doorways of the Planet – 4
The Doorways of the Planet – 5
The Days of Tomorrow
The Heart, the Ego and the Personality
The New Life That is Emerging
The Plan of Evolution and Us
The Practical Mystic
The Seventh Ray and the Devas
The Spark from the Divine Level
The Transmutation of the Logos of the Earth
The Voice of Amhaj
To Be Universal – Part 1
To Be Universal – Part 2

To Medical Doctors and Therapists
To Those Who Pray – 1
To Those Who Pray – 2
Towards Self Consecration
We are Part of the Cosmos
Working Spiritually with One's Mind
Working with the Feminine Polarity
Working with the Rays